# Head Over Wheels

# Head Over Wheels

*A Quad's Lessons from Adventures in Wheelchair Dating*

## PAT CHANG

Flipper Publishing LLP

Head Over Wheels:
A Quad's Lessons from Adventures in Wheelchair Dating

Pat Chang

Published by Flipper Publishing LLP

Copyright © 2021 by Pat Chang

All rights reserved.

Flipper Publishing LLP
93 Meyer Road, Unit 10-02
Singapore 437986

**Limit of Liability/Disclaimer of Warranty:**

Publishing and editorial team:
Author Bridge Media, www.AuthorBridgeMedia.com
Project Manager and Editorial Director: Helen Chang
Publishing Manager: Laurie Aranda

ISBN: 978-981-18-2831-7 (Paperback)
       978-981-18-2832-4 (Kindle)

**Ordering Information:**

Quantity sales. Special discounts are available on quantity purchases by corporations, associations, and others. For details, contact the publisher at the address above.

Printed in the United States of America and Singapore.

# DEDICATION

To Super Quad Daters, past, present, and future:

May you create the companion of your dreams, rise in love, and be head over wheels!

# CONTENTS

 @patschang

# The Pressure Sores of Dating

## Leopard-Print Panties

Tannia, a luscious, long-haired woman I had been dating, peeked out of my bedroom. From her index finger, she dangled another woman's satin, leopard-print panties. "What is *this*?"

Earlier, Tannia showed up with a suitcase and headed straight to my closet to make room for her things. That's when she found the underwear.

As she held it up for me to see, my heart skipped a few beats.

"Oops!" I said, as nonchalantly as I could, and then quickly wheeled myself to another room where I didn't have to face her.

As I hid in the room, I fast-forwarded through all the relationship books I had read and all the movies I had seen about dating. I rationalized what happened. *I need to project an image of a confident, happening, popular guy, right? If my new girlfriend finds the underwear of an ex-girlfriend, that tells her I've got people lined up to date me. And it makes me more desirable!*

@patschang

When I went back into the bedroom, I acted casual, like the whole thing was no big deal. *Yeah*, I kept reminding myself, *Women come to my apartment all the time. Sometimes, they leave panties or bras. So what?! I'm Pat Chang, and women love me.*

Back then, dating was a game to be won. I wanted to be seen as independent and powerful. My cavalier attitude masked my deep dating insecurities. I thought I was breaking my limits. Instead, I was pushing away real connections.

In my teens, after my accident, I never thought I'd get a girl. When you're in a wheelchair, your world grows smaller, your dreams shrinking like a leaky balloon. Dating possibilities seem particularly limited.

## Pressure Sores

For the wheelchair-bound, pressure sores develop because of habits. They can be serious (I was in bed for three months, thrice) or even life-threatening. Even after they heal, new ones will develop if habits are not changed. Good habits lead to good health without pressure sores.

Dating results are also dependent on good habits.

Whether you're a paraplegic, someone with missing limbs, or, even worse, a quad—a quadriplegic, with all four limbs affected by paralysis—it can be hard to imagine yourself as desirable.

 @patschang

You think, *Who would want to date me?*

Maybe you've got someone in mind but not enough courage to ask them out. What can you offer that's better than what others offer?

Maybe you've met people on a dating app, but after they saw your full-body photos, they ghosted you.

Maybe you've landed dates, but you wonder how to hold someone's hand or even use your hands in a romantic situation. You've read all those books about dating for able-bodied, muscular, bronze Adonises, but how do those clever techniques apply to your situation? You simply can't carry another person in your arms, throw their body on a bed, or climb on theirs.

Or maybe your relationship ended, and you blame it on the chair. You wonder if you will ever date again. Or maybe you can easily land dates, but with the wrong people.

These experiences, and the doubts they reinforce, result in pressure sores of dating: initially tiny and innocuous, but if left untreated, it becomes debilitating. However, like pressure sores on your butt, pressure sores of dating are not only treatable, they are also preventable with the right habits and mindset.

Wheelchair or not, we are all disabled in some way. Even a seemingly healthy person has some kind of disability—reasons to doubt our abilities and stop short of pursuing our dreams. But there are no limits. We are all filled with possibilities, regardless of physical limitations. We have what we need—we've always had it. We're complete. And the possibilities are endless.

I invite you on a new journey, an adventure of dating and love. It's an opportunity to transcend your wheels and let your spirit rise from the doubts of your mind—to live head over wheels. By following these lessons, you can turn your dating life into an adventure of romance, joy, and unlimited possibility.

## Super Quad Dater

Who am I to say this? I'm just a dude in a wheelchair. You might call me a super quad dater.

I'm a quadriplegic, paralyzed from my chest down. I spend most of my waking hours in a wheelchair, with a writing splint in one hand and a leg bag down one side. That has not stopped me from enjoying a robust love life. I've dated tall, sexy, beautiful women, and many became my lovers and girlfriends. Along the way, I learned lessons that expanded my life as a person, a lover, and a companion while pursuing adventures—both in and out of bed.

Although I didn't know it at the time, those seeds of insight grew into a life of joy. Those lessons served as a foundation for living: in dating, relationships, work, and business.

Eventually, I married one special woman—a stunning, gorgeous, five-foot-nine beauty named Antonia—and together, we have a young son. Together, we enjoy a life of joy, abundance, and possibilities. In my quest to inspire others, I travel the world as a speaker, author, investor, and entrepreneur.

How did a quad like me land such fantastic dates, marry the woman of my dreams, and live my dream life? The answer is simple, but it works, like preventing and treating pressure sores before they become a problem.

I created the life of my dreams by overcoming my mental blocks and focusing on what really matters: being a good companion. When I learned to be a good companion to all, I could be a good companion to any lover or wife. I no longer needed to be *head over heels* with lovers. I wanted to be *head over wheels*—gaining mastery over myself to attract the perfect companion.

## Seeds of Companionship

This book is a guide to love and life from the perspective of a quad.

As I discovered, the key to dating success lies within. For me, successful relationships start with being aware of my current mindset, which I define as a habitual way of interacting with the world, and then transforming it into the mindset of a super quad dater: the amazing companion that women find irresistible.

You don't need to "find" your soulmate, "look" for a date, or "hunt" for that perfect person. By becoming a great companion, you'll naturally attract great companions. As your companionship skills evolve, your dates will likewise become better companions.

Through my stories of quad dating, you can find inspiration. With the actions I suggest, you can start creating your own fun. Join me on my dating adventures, and you will create your own. By the end of this ride, you will see that dating is not about perfection. It is about possibilities. We've always had what we needed. We're complete, and the journey of adventure is endless.

Don't fall in love. Rise in love. Be head over wheels.

*Chapter 1*

# There's No I in Quad

I used to think being a quad was the worst kind of disability. People always assume you're like other people they've seen in wheelchairs.

"Hey, Pat," one friend would say. "Why can't you go snowboarding?"

Another would say, "Pat, why can't you go para-cycling?"

I wanted to scream.

"Those are paraplegics. I can't even use my hands!"

But I've learned that we all face challenges. We all compare ourselves to others, regardless of our abilities.

"Well, that guy has more trunk control," you might hear a paraplegic say about another. "He can do more than I can."

I spent years comparing myself to able-bodied people. I wanted to look like them, to date like them. But how? I couldn't even hold a girl's hand!

As I discovered, relationships are not just about what we do or say. They're about how we think.

Relationships are like wheelchairs: you can't get far with one wheel. You need all four. I've witnessed many great relationships that crumble because of a focus on just one wheel. Whether we are disabled or able-bodied, every

 @patschang

relationship is a balance of priorities, a merging of the *I* and the *we*. Within that balance, we create space for our relationships to grow.

## Before and After

My life divides into before and after the accident.

Before the accident, I was a competitive swimmer with washboard abs and straight-A grades. Popular and good-looking, I knew that when I grew older, dating would be easy.

At thirteen, the accident took my looks, my athleticism, and my confidence. It left me paralyzed from the chest down, with limited use of my arms and hands. After four months in rehab, I knew I would be in a wheelchair for the rest of my life.

My friends' social lives blossomed as I watched from the sidelines. *Who would want to date me?* I thought. *I wouldn't even want to date myself!* Dating wasn't even a possibility, it seemed. When my friends boasted about hooking up, I felt lonely, inadequate, and angry.

## Strategies for Lovers

In my early twenties, eager to get girls, I read all the mainstream dating books. Determined and disciplined, I decided to master their dating techniques. I wanted to prove to myself—and the world—that I was good enough.

 @patschang

But the dating experts' advice left me perplexed. How could I throw a woman on a bed—or anywhere, for that matter—when I was in a wheelchair? I couldn't even get myself into bed without help.

As much as I feared rejection and embarrassment, I dreaded being alone even more. So I adapted classic dating rituals, even hiring a dating coach (able-bodied). "The person who needs the relationship less has the power in the relationship," dating books advocated. So I projected an "I like you, but I don't *need* you" attitude. If women needed an alpha-male rock star who was fazed by nothing, that's what I'd be. Somehow.

To overcome my wheelchair, I took dates only to fancy restaurants where the staff would open the doors for us. I ordered champagne, in light glass stems, instead of beer, in heavy mugs I couldn't hold. And I strategized ways to lean in from my wheelchair for a kiss.

As I became less self-conscious and more self-assured, I discovered how to seduce women. My bedroom became a revolving door of lovers who eagerly lifted my body from my wheelchair and threw *me* onto the bed.

After a few years, the excitement of romance and sex fizzled. My relationships rarely lasted more than six months and inevitably left me feeling empty. *Why*, I wondered, *don't my relationships work out? What's the common factor?*

I realized that I sought relationships to feel whole, but because I was afraid to look weak, I hid my feelings.

I deliberately kept my emotional distance. As soon as a woman started getting serious, I pulled back, and the relationship fell apart. I was so focused on the *I* that I couldn't maintain the *we*.

## Fatal Attraction

After yet another breakup, I was so depressed and lonely that I started hunting for another woman. At a coffee shop, I chatted up a stylish woman with heavenly-white skin and molten-red lips. I got her number and asked her to meet for dinner.

I couldn't stop thinking about this raven-haired beauty. *She was gorgeous and super smart.* When we met for dinner, I was instantly infatuated. We flirted, and she mentioned her unhappy marriage.

*We could easily become lovers*, I thought. *Why not go for it? We could console each other in our loneliness.*

We met a few more times, and my attraction for her grew stronger. But I also felt something gnawing inside.

I called my sister, Michelle, and explained the situation. "Do you think it's OK for me to start dating this woman?"

The air was brisk as I wheeled myself down the sidewalk.

"If you have to ask me that question," Michelle said, "it means you already know the answer."

Her words startled me. I realized I was so desperate for a relationship that I nearly did something I knew I'd regret.

I also realized I had been focusing solely on pleasure and fun. I didn't care what would happen to her marriage or how her husband would feel. I cared only about myself. Nothing else mattered.

That night, as I watched TV, I finally realized why my relationships never succeeded. The common factor in all my failed relationships was . . . Pat.

Me.

These women didn't leave me because of my wheelchair. They had dated me, and many had slept with me, despite my disability. My problems stemmed not from the disability, but from how I thought about it. I was always trying to hide or compensate for it. I let it dominate my dating life and determine my mindset. I realized I still harbored anxiety, hurt, and anger surrounding the accident.

This revelation prompted me to gradually, painfully, let go of the bitter feelings about my disability. Although I wanted to cling to my sadness and anger, I knew that unless I changed my mindset, I would never escape the endless cycle of dating and breaking up.

I needed a new direction.

## Dating 2.0

I stopped reading dating books and started looking harder at myself. How could I find true companionship unless I turned myself into a good partner for someone?

 @patschang

Then an insight came to me: to *have* companionship, *give* companionship.

*Be* a great companion, and I will *have* a great companion.

I began focusing less on myself and my insecurities and more on my dates. Instead of trying to dazzle and impress them with my wit and charm, I listened. I spoke honestly, acted generously, and appreciated them more. Simply put, there is no *I* in quad.

In the process, I broke through my self-imposed limits and found a more satisfying way to date. And you can too. Whether you're a quad, paraplegic, or able-bodied, these principles for successful dating can work for anyone.

Becoming a better companion made my relationships more joyous and fulfilling. As I planted seeds of goodness, my dating life sprouted into happier relationships. And as I grew into a loving companion, I attracted a loving companion who became my wife.

## Adventures and Lessons

In the following chapters, I share my dating adventures and the lessons along the way. The mistakes, while painful, helped me grow. May these stories help you achieve a fulfilling dating life of romance, sex, and companionship.

I offer my insights in ten key lessons:

- **Rinse your leg bag – Clean up**: Clear your physical space to make room for a great relationship.

 @patschang

- **Weight shift the past – Release the past**: Let go of painful memories, negative thoughts, and bitter feelings, clearing the way for new and better opportunities.

- **Halo of acceptance – Accept yourself and others**: Know your value, and release negative judgment. When you do, anything seems possible.

- **Why is she feeding me? – Listen**: It took me two decades to get this one right. Careful listening opens up a whole new dimension in your relationship.

- **Rehab your speech – Speak with awareness**: Know the impact of your words. You can't build a meaningful relationship without mindful communication.

- **Get in the comfort zone – Tailor your communication**: Use an engagement style that suits your date. Watch how much better you get along when you've paid attention to this detail.

- **Honestly, do you wear a diaper? – Be honest**: Honesty opens you up to disappointments, but it also removes the limits on your relationship.

- **Ramp up generosity – Be generous**: Give freely of your heart and time. It will be repaid many times over.

- **No quickie in celebration – Persevere with joy**: Remembering to celebrate your successes, even the small ones, will infuse your relationships with joy.

- **Appreciation therapy – Appreciate**: Showing appreciation enhances your relationships and your life.

Implementing any *one* of these principles will enhance your dating experience. Implementing all ten truly transforms your life. The exercises in the chapters also give you specific actions to enhance each lesson.

Before I met Antonia, I barely practiced the lessons. Most of my effort went into changing other people's perceptions of me. That's why my relationships failed. Just as I started to work on myself, I met Antonia. I went from having zero meaningful relationships to getting engaged within 57 days of meeting the woman of my dreams.

But I was lucky. Antonia stuck with me and guided me. Until I met someone that made me want to learn these lessons, I didn't do the things I'm sharing with you in this book. But if you start now, you won't have to wait for the woman of your dreams to fix you. You'll have the tools needed to change yourself and get the relationships you want. Consistent effort will bring incredible results!

This book is not a dating techniques guide. Ultimately, it's a mindset manual. When you get that right, the techniques will flow. Also, for obvious reasons, I've changed the names, appearance, and circumstances of the women mentioned in the book. Antonia is the only exception.

## Unlimited Possibilities

Dating is not about your disability. It's about your mindset, your habitual way of interacting with the world.

But how can dating be about *your* mindset? Shouldn't it be about changing the mindset of your dates to get them to accept your disability, to go out with you, and to love you?

The most effective way to change your dates' mindsets is to change your own.

Dating success comes from transforming yourself into a super quad dater, the ultimate companion that women find irresistible. That means being a great companion everywhere and with everyone, not just when you're on dates. That practice and awareness are what will transform you into a super quad dater.

Dating, for many, is about *I*: *I* want a girl to look, behave, and make *me* feel a certain way. Yet as a super quad dater, the focus is on being the best companion by bringing joy, fun, acceptance, and connection to your dates. With a mindful approach, you are a companion to your date and to the other people in your lives.

There is no *I* in a super quad dater.

 @patschang

Are you worried that you need to start pleasing people—even lose your identity—just to get dates?

A super quad dater doesn't need to worry about pleasing. He has great qualities, and people love to be around him. He draws others to him with his positivity, big heart, kindness, authenticity, and generosity.

To become a super quad dater, you don't need anything except an open mind and a willing heart.

It starts with something as simple as rinsing your leg bag.

*Chapter 2*

# Rinse Your Leg Bag

## Clutter Blindness

Sometimes we can't see our own blind spots. Prior to meeting Antonia, I didn't think I was messy.

I was based in Beijing, while she was based in Singapore. We met in Beijing, introduced by mutual friends. Although she left a deep impression, I didn't contact her. A long-distance relationship would require too much effort.

A year and a half later, we met again in Shanghai at our mutual friends' wedding. This time, sparks flew. By the time I was on my way to the airport, we were exchanging flirty messages. To my surprise, she said she was interested in visiting me in the US.

I made her travel arrangements and jokingly suggested that, as her travel agent, I would arrange for her to stay at my apartment. I thought she would reject my flirty comment—after all, we had only met a few times.

But Antonia surprised me by agreeing to stay at my place. I couldn't believe my good fortune! I quickly began tidying. I organized, dusted, vacuumed, and emptied a can

 @patschang

of Febreze over several days to let the sweet vanilla scent soak into my apartment.

By the time I picked her up, my apartment had looked—and smelled—amazing. *This is an epic story I'll tell my grandkids*, I thought in disbelief, barely able to contain my excitement.

I didn't expect Antonia's reaction when she stepped inside my front door.

"Wow, Pat. I didn't know you lived in a storage container," she said.

Huh?

She pointed out that my kitchen counter and coffee table were covered in mail, my dining room table was invisible, piled with magazines and books, and my closet was overflowing. I was completely oblivious! I'm fortunate that she saw past my clutter to the real me.

Cleaning up can be literal, like wiping down the wheels of your wheelchair. But it's also about cleaning the clutter of old relationships, of the things holding you back. Cleaning up provides you with clarity about the kind of relationship you want and the ability to make it happen. Cleaning up opens the doors to adventures in wheelchair dating, romance, and life.

## Don't Mess with Success

I've been messy since my early teens. I didn't see the value in cleaning up, and it got progressively worse as I got older. My parents never enforced tidiness, and after the accident, they became even more lenient. I justified my messiness with my wheelchair. *I'm paralyzed from the chest down*, I reasoned. *I have bigger problems to deal with. My attendant can clean up.*

A young man living alone, I didn't see my own mess. If my attendant did a reasonable job, and I had a clean shirt and combed hair, that was enough. *I am not messy*, I told myself. *I just cannot tidy up because of my wheelchair.* Even my leg bag, which held my urine as I sat in the wheelchair, often went uncleaned in my bathroom. Cleaning was a hassle, so I learned to tolerate my messiness. Eventually, I became blind to it: I literally did not notice my own clutter.

Over time, I discovered that when your environment is neat and organized, you function better and think more clearly. Your space gives off a welcoming and positive energy. That's a major turn-on for both you and your date. Conversely, clutter can hinder you and cloud your thinking. It also turns people off, especially potential romantic partners who are imagining sharing a space with you.

The physical space you inhabit reflects who you are and your state of mind. Imagine going to Yosemite National Park and finding trash all over the ground! The park would lose its magnificence and allure.

Whether your clutter exists in your physical world or in the virtual space of your computer and phone, it impacts your mind and spirit. It can trap you in the past, not allowing you to move forward freely into new experiences.

## 10 Ways to Clean Your Room and Turn It into A Sex Den

1. Ask your buddy to polish your bathroom mirror. Your hot date doesn't want to see food bits sprayed onto it from flossing!

2. Roll up the blinds and allow natural light to lift the space's frequency. It should not feel like a prisoner's cell in a dungeon.

3. Lay a new underpad on your bed. Your date's bare bottom should not be touching yellow polka dots.

4. Do not pile mail on countertops or tabletops.

5. Dispose of all unused gadgets and electronics. Your sex den is not a repair shop.

6. Wash your urinal thoroughly (I recommend dishwashing soap), and make sure it's scent-free.

7. Wash your urine bags and catheters, so they don't have build-up.

 @patschang

8.  Toss out expired food in the refrigerator. I kept grapes until they turned into raisins!

9.  Have Haagen-Dazs (for before, during, and after sex!) and three choices of tea on hand.

10. Prepare a flask of filtered water.

    When you clean your space, the new will flow in. When you clean your bed, you make space for new lovers.

## A Messy Past

Hoarding stuff was a major weakness for me. It got to the point that girlfriends were offended, and my relationships suffered.

One rainy night, my date and I sat in the dining room, eating dinner. I usually eat in my office, so I hadn't taken stock of my dining room decor in a while. Imagine my horror when I looked at the walls and saw pictures of me with my ex-girlfriend. Not just one picture, but multiple photos everywhere! My date didn't say anything, but I felt uneasy the entire night and could not enjoy her company.

I told myself that hanging on to old mementos or pictures made me a romantic. Sometimes I even convinced myself it made me more attractive to women because they would see that I had options. But all it really did was keep me stuck in a rut.

I couldn't see beyond my clutter into my future.

The experience made me think. Sure, I can rationalize that with a disability, it's hard to clean my physical environment. But leaving old photos on the wall or keeping a camera full of pictures of an ex? The wheelchair was an excuse. My clutter was my own.

## Polish Your Hardware

People with disabilities and special needs almost always come with equipment. Taking pride in maintaining the devices you use to function can boost your confidence and create a better impression.

One day, on my way to a friend's house, I got caught in the rain. When I rolled into his foyer, my wheels left dark streaks on the carpet. What a wake-up call! I had used that chair for seven years and never once washed it. I decided then and there that I would take pride in the appearance of my wheelchair the same way I did my own appearance.

The same thing goes for my leg bag. I ignored it whenever possible because it embarrassed me. But if I don't clean my leg bag, it will leak, get dirty, and maybe even cause an infection. Despite how much I hated it, cleaning my leg bag was a key part of keeping me clean, presentable, and healthy.

 @patschang

## Don't Do It Like a Porn Star

I used to have a secret porn folder on my laptop. Whenever anyone borrowed my laptop, I felt nervous. *What if she finds my secret stash?*

Yes, I watched porn. I thought it was my right as a man to watch it. Besides, there are worse vices!

But then I stopped. Watching porn wasn't a habit that would help me reach my goals. I didn't even feel good after watching it, which was whenever I was really bored, stressed, or upset at my girlfriend.

Watching porn did not improve my dating life. It just gave me all kinds of unrealistic expectations of how sex should be, and it made me frustrated when my girlfriend was not doing it like a porn star.

That might be true for you too. Unless, of course, your girlfriend is a porn star.

But even if your girlfriend is a porn star or likes to watch porn (which most guys probably think is a dream come true), I still suggest you delete your porn and stop watching it.

"Why???" you ask. Let me assure you: nothing turns you off faster than seeing a hairy, 12-inch cock on your girlfriend's computer screen, right?

The same is true when she sees images of other naked women on your screen. No matter how well you think your porn is hidden, it clutters your mind.

> If you're serious about cleaning your space, say goodbye to your porn stash. It's another way to clean your mind and space while welcoming real intimacy.
>
> Press "Delete" for hotter sex!

## Outside In

I could see that my external mess had caused an internal, emotional reaction. The clutter made me less focused and more closed off to new things. This is because our world is a mirror: the world we live in reflects ourselves.

This is not philosophical musing. Who bought the furniture, left piles of letters on the countertop, selected the posters on the wall, and hung the clothes in the closet? I did.

My environment is a reflection of me. It is the cumulative, physical manifestation of my thoughts and actions. I used to repeat to myself, *I'm disabled. My life is messy and hard.* That mantra manifested in my living environment: messy and full of obstacles.

The thoughts we repeat become a reality.

Taking steps to clean up my messes and clear out my spaces reflected back to me. My mind became clearer, and I felt more effective and more attractive.

Change your environment, and you will change.

The messes in my life were also imprisoning me in the past, which made me less present for my current relationships.

 @patschang

Removing the evidence of those failed relationships freed me of my old cycle of dating. I could visualize more clearly a different, better kind of relationship.

A clean environment will result in a clear mind. A clear mind knows what it wants and how to get it.

## Don't Skip It

Clearing big messes is hard work. I needed a wake-up call to realize I had a problem.

This is that call for you.

Can you see your countertops? Has your date ever found a picture or piece of clothing from an old relationship? Are your aids and devices in good, clean order? What are the dirty leg bags in your life?

When I first began tidying up, I complained about how hard and time-consuming it was. I felt hostile toward my "junk." Every time I threw something away, I experienced grief. But it was necessary.

If you think you might be blind to clutter like I was, ask a close friend to help. Cleaning up your environment will not only make you more successful in dating, it will also make you more successful in life. Think of it as making space for your next great relationship, like clearing land to plant a garden.

When I experienced the "rebirth" of my apartment, I learned what decluttering isn't. Decluttering isn't about throwing things away, having few possessions, or living frugally. And it isn't just about appearance either. It's about having a deep appreciation for what you already have. Yes, including your wheelchair and your leg bag.

For me, decluttering was about acknowledging and appreciating my past and then letting it go. When you're disposing of pictures of your ex-girlfriends, do so with kindness and gratitude. Your past relationships, even bad ones, shaped you and helped you grow. Say "Thank you" and let them go.

*Chapter 3*

# Weight Shift the Past

## Ditched at a Wedding

Sometimes failure can hold us back. In my early twenties, at a friend's wedding, I spotted a stunning brunette in a glittering, pink sequin dress, her soft curls draped over her bare right shoulder. *Who is SHE?* We made eye contact and exchanged flirty smiles as the courses were being served.

Later she sauntered over with her dessert plate. "Would you like to share this chiffon cake with me?"

*OH! The heat just turned up a notch!* Her slender arm resting on mine, Rachel and I talked easily between bites, sharing laughs and inappropriate jokes. Music started, and the bride and groom danced the first song. Wedding guests soon joined in.

Someone came over to our table, where we were now sitting by ourselves, and asked Rachel to dance. She beamed and jumped up. Hand in hand, they walked away.

I was crushed.

 @patschang

I didn't know how to dance in my wheelchair, and I was too embarrassed to try. Whenever I pictured myself doing it, I looked like a fool.

*This is how my life will be,* I thought. *Every time I find a great girl, the wheelchair will get in the way.* If I weren't in this chair, I'd have dates lined up. *I* would be the one whisking women away from their conversations onto the dance floor.

I couldn't let go of how that night had made me feel. Almost a decade would pass before I tried dancing in my chair.

Focusing on the past is like sitting too long without doing weight shifts. A wheelchair user must shift body weight to redistribute weight and prevent pressure sores. As a super quad dater, you have to weight shift your past to move forward and prevent dating pressure sores. But past failures can dictate the future. This destructive pattern keeps you from growing. If you let go of those failures, your past doesn't define you, and you open yourself up to infinite possibilities, the relationship you truly deserve, and the romantic adventure of a lifetime.

## Disability Doesn't Define You

In my early twenties, I identified myself with my wheelchair. Everything I couldn't achieve—from daily tasks to dating—I blamed on the wheelchair. I beat myself up for

 @patschang

the simple things I couldn't do, creating a huge amount of insecurity.

How I saw myself dictated my thinking and behavior. If I thought the wheelchair prevented me from doing something, I would accept it, and familiar negative feelings would surface, stopping me from trying new things.

In dating, I was guilty of repeating what was comfortable and safe. Yet that same reliable routine was producing a reliable result: failed relationships.

I needed to disentangle my past and pursue a different result. You can do this too. Take a hard look at how you've framed your past. Be honest with yourself and forgiving of others.

## Story or Truth?

Sometimes the stories we tell ourselves about the past aren't true. I had convinced myself I was perfect in every other way. The inability to dance with Rachel was what had squelched her interest. It was black and white: Pat is great; Pat in a wheelchair is a disaster.

The wheelchair was all of me, not just one aspect of me. It became my defense mechanism: when things go wrong, it's easier to blame the inanimate object than yourself.

I blamed my wheelchair for losing the beautiful Rachel to a dance partner. But perhaps she was bored with our conversation. If things fizzled out with a woman,

I blamed it on my difficulty getting on the bed after our date the night before. But maybe she just wasn't attracted to me.

After some soul-searching, I admitted that the wheelchair was only one of many things someone might not like about me.

## Update Your Beliefs

The beliefs you think are true or were once true, but are not, hold you back. It's time to replace them with new, empowering ones.

Examples of outdated beliefs:

- I can't get dates because I am in a wheelchair;
- Guys in wheelchairs can't dance;
- It is difficult to raise a family when I'm in a wheelchair.

Choose new, empowering beliefs:

- People in wheelchairs date fun, beautiful, and caring women!
- People in wheelchairs are great dancers!
- People in wheelchairs make awesome parents.

Exercise:

1. List your negative dating beliefs.

2. Turn them into powerful, positive beliefs.

Stick the new beliefs on your bathroom mirror, and repeat them to yourself daily until they become second nature!

## Forgive

Shedding the negativity of our past involves forgiving those who've rejected us.

It used to anger me when someone turned me down or broke up with me. But no one can choose who it is they like or love.

Sometimes our childhood or personality influences who attracts us, but often it can't be explained. And we will likely change our minds about people as we go through life.

If someone rejects you, they probably weren't out to hurt you. They were just the wrong person at the wrong time.

I was surprised to learn that the person who rejected me the most was me. It took me years to hear my self-criticism. Forgiving myself took even longer, but to heal fully, I had to.

### Let It Go, Let It Go

In the Hawaiian practice of forgiveness and healing, called Ho'oponopono, a person says a series of sentences to let go of past hurts:

- I'm sorry.

- I love you.

- Please forgive me.

- Thank you.

Saying these to yourself is a powerful way to heal.

## Freedom of Movement

Years after that deflating experience at the wedding, a friend told me about a family that had been in a tragic car accident. The son died, the father became a quadriplegic, and the daughter survived unharmed. I looked up the news article as I was curious about the daughter's experience being raised by a quadriplegic father. What I found was a heartwarming article and video.

The father, Paul, loved dancing with his kids, but the accident ended that. When his daughter, Brittany, was planning her wedding, she asked Paul to share a wedding dance. He reluctantly agreed, not knowing how he would dance.

@patschang

A few weeks prior to the wedding, Paul and Brittany hired a choreographer who specialized in teaching dance to the wheelchair-bound. I watched, over and over, the video of them dancing at the wedding. The sight moved me to tears: Paul, elegant and effortless in his chair, dancing along with his daughter and directing her when she became too emotional.

Paul hadn't danced in 17 years.

That brave father taught me something: it's possible to dance beautifully in a wheelchair, and to do so with joy.

A year later, at a neighbor's wedding, I danced in my wheelchair.

## Create Your Perfect Date

Once you clear the past, you have room to create your future, including your perfect future date. First, choose three qualities you desire in a date. Here are mine:

- Caring
- Cheerful
- Beautiful

Be truthful. If you want a girl who starts French kissing you within thirty minutes of meeting you, put it down (more on this later). Be careful what you wish for because you will get it.

For each of the three qualities, come up with a place where *you* can provide the quality to *others*. But before we continue further, I want to discuss *Beautiful*.

Beautiful is what many guys want but don't say. I was one of them.

Qualities such as caring and cheerful are causes (as in "cause and effect"). By developing these qualities yourself, you create the cause for things (effects) to happen. For example, by being caring ("cause"), you attract someone who is caring ("effect").

Beauty, however, is an effect, *not* a cause.

To have an effect, you must have a cause.

So what is the cause for beauty?

Patience! (Think about girls taking A WHILE getting ready to go somewhere!) Patience is the root cause for beauty (and other good things).

If you want to date beautiful girls, develop patience.

Let's go back to the example:

- Caring – hospital
- Cheerful – uplifting others
- ~~Beautiful~~ Patience – party

To become caring, I volunteered at hospitals and spoke at a local rehab center. For cheerful, I attended a spiritual center where I feel uplifted, and I uplift others. For patience—the cause for beauty—I chose party.

That's right! Party! I practiced patience by dressing up and looking sharp!

You can develop great qualities almost anywhere. Be creative. Just remember you must provide to others whatever quality you want.

If you want to meet girls who will kiss you within thirty minutes of meeting you, reflect on the cause for this effect. Is it being accepting? Non-judging? Go to a place where this quality occurs frequently, and practice this quality yourself.

You don't need to spend much time there. Start with 30 minutes a week. Consistency is the key.

You will meet people with the qualities you want in your dates at places where these qualities are being provided. Get to know these awesome people. Practice providing these qualities. You may not meet your dream girl, but these people may know someone with the qualities you demonstrate and desire, and introduce you.

Where we go and what we do have an enormous impact on whom we end up dating. Do this exercise with confidence and persistence, and let it surprise you with amazing results!

## Move Forward

Releasing the past can be painful. We often carry memories like a security blanket, using the knowledge of past failures to cocoon us from pain. But what we're really doing is closing ourselves off from possibilities, experiences, and potentially greater success.

If what you've been doing isn't working, don't cling to it. Take a hard look at yourself. Test your dated beliefs. Open yourself up to the idea that someone will find you attractive despite your disability because you are so much more than that one thing.

When I dance now, I think about my old self, who lived with so many self-imposed rules. I had made my world small in a misguided effort to protect myself. Letting go of that old identity opened me to the possibility of deep, meaningful relationships.

We all judge our past, for better or worse, and reach conclusions that define our mindset. But you can break that cycle of judgment to achieve freedom and joy.

*Chapter 4*

# Halo of Acceptance

## The Beast

*Beauty and the Beast* is my favorite movie. When I first watched it, I felt like the Beast character was based on me. I had everything when I was young: a loving, prosperous family, popularity, talent, and looks. I could also be insensitive, even a bully, to my classmates. Like the prince in the movie, I had everything my heart desired, but I was spoiled, selfish, and unkind.

As punishment, I became a beast—a quadriplegic in a wheelchair. At one point in the movie, the narrator says of the Beast, "As the years passed, he fell into despair and lost all hope. For who could ever learn to love a beast?" I asked myself the same question.

It was easy for me to believe the right woman would save me.

The movie's happy ending gave me hope. I didn't believe true love would restore my mobility, but I did think it would profoundly uplift my life. Just as Belle saw the goodness in the Beast, someone would see past my curse—my wheelchair—and love the real me.

 @patschang

For years I chased after that special someone who could accept and love me. I didn't know that all along I had the power to break the spell: accept the Beast and love him.

If I could not accept myself, how could anyone else accept me?

And that was a journey I still had to take.

## What Do You See in the Mirror?

Sometimes I wonder how I managed to get through any dates at all, considering how unaccepting I was about myself. *Why would anyone want to be with me, given my disability?* I viewed every date, every relationship, even live-in girlfriends, as the longest of long shots. I assumed my wheelchair would ultimately be the death of the relationship.

Once I did start dating, I adopted the philosophy that whoever needs the relationship less has all the power. I didn't call too much. I didn't spend too much time together. I continued to flirt to show her I had other options. I waited until I was certain I would not get rejected before I asked someone out.

Years after high school, my sister, Michelle, came to visit me at Stanford. During one of our late-night chats, she casually said, "Why didn't you ask Belle out? She really liked you." Belle was one of the prettiest girls in our high school. I was so shocked I couldn't speak.

"She didn't think you would be into her, so she didn't try," Michelle said.

The girl I thought I had *zero* chance with liked me? What did she see in me that I was too scared to see in myself?

For the first time, I began to see that others didn't see me the way I saw myself. If I couldn't learn to accept who I was, I would lose out on so many opportunities.

## Magical Pickup Line

Many guys want to know the "right" thing to say to a girl to get her number.

Magic is definitely involved.

But it is not a line.

*You* are the magic.

When you wear the halo of self-acceptance, your natural magic glows.

The power of persuasion comes from being truthful. When you truly, authentically embrace and love yourself, others will accept and love you too. You will be irresistible. Your words won't even matter.

This is why the same pickup line, delivered by different people, produces different results.

Now let's create a magical pickup line:

- Remember your motivation: you are practicing the qualities of a great companion, not picking up women.

- Keep it simple: long, elaborate lines sound rehearsed and are hard to deliver smoothly.

- Be honest: don't make up stories just to arouse her interest.

- Release expectations: relax and know you have nothing to lose; if you worry about getting rejected because of your wheelchair, rejection will happen (and not because of the wheelchair).

- Don't comment on her looks, especially in a suggestive or sexual way: "You're hot" and "you're beautiful" are off-limits. Even if she's ready to jump on top of you in your chair, at least put some effort and creativity into foreplay!

Here are examples of what to say at your friend Joe's party:

1. "Hi! I'm Pat. How do you know Joe?"

2. "Hi! I love your bracelet. It's so iconic!" (Notice something specific about her—shoes, jewelry, hair. She will respond to your statement.)

3. "Wow! The black-pepper smoked duck is really smoky."

4. "Have some Dom Perignon/Chocolate Therapy (a Ben & Jerry's ice cream flavor)." Bring a bottle

of wine or dessert and offer it to everyone, not just hot girls. The wine/dessert does not need to be expensive as long as you like it and can share your enthusiasm.

Be relaxed, fun, and engaging. Be present and generous, and you will be noticed.

## Hiding Online

Learning to like myself was a long process, and it didn't happen all at once. When online dating became popular, I thought it would help me avoid the judgment of in-person meetings. (This was before we had dating sites for disabled people). If someone could get to know me before they saw my wheelchair, I might have an easier time.

I thoughtfully crafted a profile using my height (when I'm standing), humbly highlighting my career and academic achievements. Without offering my photo, the site sent me matches. I began messaging with several women, and eventually, that turned into phone calls. One woman, Adrienne, stood out. We had amazing phone conversations. Just listening to her angelic voice made my heart sing.

I knew Adrienne was striking based on her profile pictures. In one picture, she was playing the cello in an orchestra, wearing an elegant black dress and bright red lipstick.

As we continued to talk, I became more and more anxious about revealing my disability. Surely she wondered why I hadn't shared photos of myself. I invented excuses when she suggested meeting in person, even turning down an invitation to see her perform.

Finally, it became too awkward to explain why I didn't want to meet. Rather than go through certain rejection, I stopped calling. I disappeared from her life, hurting us both. That decision made me miserable, and I regretted it. But I was so sure she wouldn't accept my limitations—because I hadn't embraced them myself.

## What's Normal?

We have a hard time accepting ourselves because we've constructed, over our lifetimes, this idea of "normal." We think there's a normal way to look, a normal way to act, a normal way to date.

If there's one thing I've learned from dating as a disabled person, it's that normal doesn't exist.

One of my major concerns in dating centered around the bed. In movies, men scoop up women and toss them onto the bed, then climb on top. Where to even start with this one! I can't get into bed without assistance, and I absolutely can't lift someone else into bed.

Once, after a fun evening, I brought a date back to my place. The lighthearted bantering picked up and became

 @patschang

increasingly suggestive. We'd been kissing, and we both felt it was time to move to the bed. Nervous but excited, we went into my bedroom. I positioned my wheelchair next to the bed. My date stood in front of me and attempted to pull me toward the bed.

I barely budged.

I'm five feet, ten inches tall when I'm standing, so I'm not tiny. Undeterred, my date, from behind, wrapped her hands around my chest and pulled. I didn't move. After a few more attempts, she collapsed onto the bed while I hung my head in defeat.

I didn't know where to turn for advice. I was too embarrassed to talk to my friends, and I didn't think they could help. After all, they weren't in wheelchairs. I thought about all kinds of solutions—wearing a buttonless shirt I could take off myself, removing the tray on my chair to get physically closer, and denying myself liquids to lower the risk of needing my leg bag emptied.

None of those solutions worked. They weren't natural. Forcing an able-bodied norm onto my body and my lifestyle was unrealistic. In desperation, I enlisted the help of a dating coach to figure out how to make intimacy with a date smoother and more "normal." The coach helped me understand that my own normal was okay.

I had to stop judging and do what worked for me.

Eventually, I asked dates to remove my shirt for me. They found this sexy! And once I could clearly and confidently explain the technique for getting me into bed, almost any woman could do it.

---

### Turn Yourself from Beast to Prince

Feeling like a Beast? These exercises can turn you into a prince.

Beast to Prince, part 1

Plant a seed of accepting yourself by writing a note to yourself. Apologize for judging yourself. Thank yourself for being wonderful and awesome. With appreciation, feed the note into a shredder.

Beast to Prince, part 2

Plant a seed of accepting others by writing a note to someone else. Apologize for judging that person. Feed the note into a shredder. For a more powerful experience, deliver the note in person.

Beast to Prince, part 3

Sit normally in front of a full-length mirror (available at most clothing retailers) or reflective glass door. Take a picture (ask a friend or use the timer). Are you slouching? Are your shoulders even? Are your pant legs the same length? Adjust your posture, and sit straight and tall. Does it feel awkward? Practice sitting this way until it becomes natural.

---

Beast to Prince, part 4

Create an online dating profile with photos that represent you truthfully. Don't emphasize the wheelchair, but don't hide it either. In your bio, avoid sweeping statements like "I love to travel"—unless you truly do and can support the statement. Do you work in the travel industry? Organize tours? Or did you really mean you love vacations? Be specific—and honest.

## The Eye of the Beholder

After many dates, it finally sunk in that I wasn't a beast to anyone but myself. If a woman said yes to a date, she had probably already accepted me.

My confidence grew, and I asked out more women. Sometimes I struck out, but often they agreed, eroding my walls of self-judgment. I became more comfortable, less worried about how I looked or how I navigated the world in my wheelchair.

Acceptance often comes when you begin to really understand a person. Like Belle and the Beast, it takes time to grow comfortable with each other—or yourself. The best way to really understand your date, not surprisingly, is to listen.

*Chapter 5*

# Why Is She Feeding Me?

## Big Talker

We met for the first time at dinner in Beijing. I was living there, and she was there for business. This bright-eyed, long-haired beauty had a friend whose boyfriend happened to be my friend, and he invited me to join their group for dinner. My girlfriend was busy, so I went alone. Besides, I never say no to Peking duck.

When she walked in and introduced herself, I was immediately struck. Tall and fair, she was physically striking. She was fluent in both English and Chinese, and her quirky sense of humor fascinated me. We spent the whole night talking. When she mentioned she was in Beijing for three days, I invited myself to all her dinners, as I was familiar with the restaurants and could order local favorites.

We spent the next three nights eating out with our friends. At each meal, she did something unusual: she fed me. All through dinner, she would take forkfuls of food from my plate and feed me. It seemed flirty and affectionate. *She must really like me*, I thought.

 @patschang

The timing wasn't right for us then, and we exchanged contact information but didn't keep in touch. Several years later, when we were both single, we started a relationship. I asked her what she had thought of me all those years ago. I expected to hear something about my intelligence, sense of humor, charm, or good looks.

"I thought you were annoying," she admitted with a laugh.

"That can't be!" I protested, genuinely shocked. "If you didn't like me, why did you keep feeding me at dinner?"

"It was the only way to stop you from talking!"

This revelation jarred me. I thought my ability to converse was a strength. Believing my disability held me back, I leaned heavily on my personality, confidence, charm, and humor. Now I knew I had become overconfident. I talked too much, annoying the woman I was trying to impress.

Because of her honesty, I discovered I needed to listen more. The woman who taught me this lesson, the one who fed me Peking duck to shut me up, was Antonia, who honored me by becoming my wife.

Listening is about connecting with another person. As protagonists of our own stories, we tend to be very focused on *I*. Listening helps us be aware of a whole other world, the *we* possibilities.

## Make a Connection

Talking Antonia's head off at dinner came from an urge to share everything with this wonderful, beautiful woman. I loved seeing her reactions to my words, the feeling of power that came from impressing her. Looking back, it's obvious how selfish and shortsighted that was.

Talking instead of listening is a common mistake, especially for those trying to make a good impression. You think your funny stories and thought-provoking observations will get someone to fall for you. And when you add a disability to the mix, it's natural to lean on what you see as your strengths. But all that talking can backfire. You can wind up labeled as annoying, pompous, or self-centered.

While talking too much irritates people, listening and asking questions builds respect and connection. Nothing makes a person think more highly of you than when you show her you care about what she says.

If you remember you're good enough as you are, it's easier to relax and listen, rather than try to impress. Perhaps you're a better talker than listener, but everyone can get better at listening, and you can continue to improve over the lifetime of your relationships.

## Listen Your Way to Style

Get a style upgrade! At a new-to-you shopping center, look for a woman whose style you like (*not* because she's hot!). Ask her to recommend a men's clothing store there, as it's your first time there. Answer any questions about the occasion you're shopping for or your preferred style. Thank her sincerely and find the store she suggests. You may need to talk to a few women before one will give you a recommendation.

At the store, ask a saleswoman whose style you like (again, *not* because she's hot!) to put together an outfit. Practice listening and asking questions—and sit confidently! If you like the outfit she recommends, try it on. For wheelchair users, pay attention to the fit of the suit jacket and tighter fitting pants. Shirts from American designers such as Ralph Lauren tend to have larger armholes, while shirts from European designers such as Ted Baker tend to be slimmer. When you put on the suit jacket, make sure there is no collar gap. The pants should not be tight around the crotch.

If you look good in the outfit, buy it.

This exercise enhances your listening skills. If you go to a woman that you find hot for your style upgrade, you will not be able to listen to her or practice this essential skill. Focus on developing your skills, and dates will follow.

## Use It or Lose It

Consistent, close listening can be a struggle, especially if you're a big talker like me. When you click with someone, you want to talk even more. So how do you rein yourself in?

Being aware is half the battle. If you're prone to talking, check yourself periodically. Have you asked a question in the last five minutes? When your date answers a question, rather than launch into *your* take on the subject, pause, look into her eyes, then re-engage. You're excited about this person, so let yourself be interested in every aspect of who she is! But also keep the conversation balanced: asking too many questions can turn a conversation into an interview.

Without mindful listening, how will you know what foods your date likes, what she does for fun, or details about her family? Gathering information by listening will provide insight into what kind of person your date is—what inspires her and motivates her.

Listening is a skill. To become better at this skill, you need to practice. Listen all the time, not just on dates. Don't fall into the trap of feeling like you're listening only to get something. If you practice listening in all aspects of your life, it will become second nature, and your relationships will progress easily to the next stage.

## A Breakup and a Breakthrough

You may wonder how in the world I convinced Antonia to marry me after I blew my first impression. The answer is Sophie, the person I was dating when I first met Antonia in Beijing.

From the start, my relationship with Sophie was rocky. I talked too much—obviously—and I didn't listen well. Sophie complained that I flirted with other women and was unfaithful, which was true. She wanted to settle down, but I wasn't ready to commit.

I brushed aside Sophie's complaints and invested little time in getting to know her. This pompous attitude really came from my continuing insecurity. I wanted to be the one who needed the relationship less. It made me feel powerful and in control. I flirted openly to let her know that I had options. I wanted to dominate the relationship.

After a year, Sophie and I broke up. The breakup felt especially painful because it was clear to me how poorly I had treated her. She was a loving, kind, and caring person. I hadn't listened, and I was disrespectful of her feelings. Rather than actively listening and addressing her concerns, I avoided issues until they exploded. I knew I needed to do better.

The next time I saw Antonia, at a wedding in Shanghai, almost two years had passed since our first meeting. Antonia says she noticed the difference in me. No longer the egotistical talker, I listened more. I was present and engaged. She no longer needed to feed me forkfuls of food just to shut me up. Antonia was heartened to see I was capable of change. At that wedding, it clicked for her that I was the one.

Sometimes our worst failures lead to the best progress. If I hadn't messed things up so badly with Sophie, I might not have been the person I became to attract Antonia.

---

### Shut Me Up with Your Mouth

While having a conversation on a date, for five minutes, say only the following:

- I appreciate you.
- You are awesome.
- That's amazing.
- Tell me more.

Plant a seed of understanding by listening.

---

## Keep Listening

Listening acts like glue to hold a relationship together.

Because Antonia looks like a model and dresses well, I assumed she had expensive taste. Initially, I took her to the trendiest restaurants I could find. I thought if I took her

@patschang

to casual places, she might be disappointed in my lack of sophistication and financial resources.

But when she visited me in Beijing, she would take a walk in the morning and bring back Chinese pancakes from a street vendor. She loved those pancakes. It surprised me because I had this image of her as a high-end-restaurant person. I made an incorrect assumption because I didn't listen. If I had asked Antonia what types of food or restaurants she liked, I could have created better dates for her.

When you think you have someone figured out, that's your red flag. Do you really know that person? It takes hours of mindful listening to know someone well.

I always knew I wanted to share my life with someone, but it took me years to understand this reciprocal equation: you give, and you receive. Information, feelings, thoughts, and dreams pass between you as you talk and listen.

Listening is a relationship superpower that makes you an amazing partner. If you know someone's backstory, their fears, joys, and aspirations, you'll be much more understanding. Relationships where both partners really understand each other are kinder and deeper.

Now that you understand the profound impact of listening, it's important to think about how you speak. I didn't just learn how to listen—I learned how to stop making conversation all about me.

*Chapter 6*

# Rehab Your Speech

## Lobby Fumble

I haven't always known how to ask for what I want.

Things were going well after several dates with Jordan, a sweet and curious grad student. One night, after hugging goodbye in my apartment building lobby, I said, "I'll call you."

Jordan murmured something, turned to leave, then stopped in her tracks and turned back to me, "How come you're not asking me up to your place?" She looked hurt.

Of course, I had wanted her to come up! But I didn't have the confidence to ask her. Instead, I made her feel confused, even undesirable. Caught off guard, I muddled the situation further by telling her I would next week.

My fear of failure had turned into a self-fulfilling prophecy. I convinced myself she wasn't ready to come up, and when she volunteered, I got flustered. My mind raced through all my previous dates and good-night kisses. Cringing, I wondered how many of those women were confused why I hadn't asked them up.

 @patschang

The incident with Jordan was frustrating. My inability to speak up and my poor communication hurt both of us. From then on, I resolved, I would say what I meant, rather than letting my insecurity rule.

Quads typically undergo physical therapy, occupational therapy, and other types of rehab. But it's also important to rehab our speech. Speaking mindfully and skillfully isn't easy, but it's the cornerstone to every healthy relationship.

## Parts of Speech

I should have been honest about wanting Jordan to come up to my apartment. I also should have been more intentional with her. Just saying "I'll call you" didn't reflect my real feelings. It didn't respect her either because it left her wondering where I stood.

Speaking honestly doesn't mean you should say whatever's on your mind. That would be tactless—a turnoff. But when your thoughts and feelings are positive, it's crucial to speak your truth, even if it scares you to be transparent with your date. On the flip side, avoid speech that's negative. It serves no constructive purpose. Especially when you're first getting to know someone, negativity can be a real turnoff.

In my study of Buddhism, I learned about the four kinds of non-virtuous speech. These categories serve as a good guide for what to avoid in dating.

**Harsh speech**: speaking with intent to harm; sarcasm

**Divisive speech**: speaking with intent to create disharmony; arguing

**Idle chatter**: speaking with no intention to act; empty words or promises

**Lying**: speaking with intent to misrepresent

To put these in positive terms, it's best to speak in a genuine and upbeat way, match your words to your actions, and speak honestly. Speaking with awareness helps you avoid the catty game-playing that sometimes happens in dating. Plus, it's a major turn-on.

I'm a firm believer that what you say comes back to you. So when you speak harshly or lie, that plants seeds of negativity in your own life. In contrast, thoughtful, authentic speech sends positivity into your world that will help your relationships flourish.

### Rose-Gold Compliment

During a party, I met an elegantly dressed girl and offered a creative and effective compliment: "I like your bracelet. It's iconic." I then asked a question I knew she'd answer: "Is it rose gold?"

I got a date.

Here's your exercise: Notice something you like in a woman. Compliment her, creatively and sincerely. End with a question that will draw her into a conversation.

Don't focus on appearance. "You're hot" or "you're beautiful" is unoriginal and overused. Notice the details: her clothes, accessories, energy. Be observant, and choose one detail to compliment.

## Harsh and Divisive Speech

Aren't positive people great to spend time with? Their positivity is an almost physical warmth. It makes you want to be near them.

And then there are the negative people, who act like complaining is their primary form of communication. Who wants to be around that negativity all the time? It's a downer. Negativity is often a knee-jerk response to a difficult situation. But if you can stop the sour comment, pause, and speak with awareness, you'll create a better, more constructive outcome.

Let's say you go to a restaurant, and the service is slow. If you complain to your date, it dampens the whole mood. And what does it accomplish? It's not going to improve your service or erase the bad experience. It only makes things worse and deepens the negative imprint.

I've railed against bad servers in the past. Now I take a minute and consciously choose my response. Maybe you

 @patschang

and your date are having a great time regardless of the service, and nothing needs to be said. If the poor service is the elephant in the room, you could joke about it or give a measured comment: "Such slow service tonight! But it's busy, and our server looks slammed. This way, our date will last even longer."

Even better, tell the server you can see it's a tough night, but you would appreciate some help. If your intention is to be constructive, not to give your waiter hell, you'll receive something better back. Maybe the server works a bit harder to get you your food quickly, or maybe he just shows sincere gratitude for your understanding.

You've offered your server kindness during a hard time, and you've impressed your date by showing compassion. Everyone benefits.

## Mean What You Say

One way to practice positive speech is by doing what you say you will do. For people in wheelchairs, one excellent exercise is simply being on time.

For this exercise, make an appointment somewhere. Get there on time. Do this with friends and family, then with dates.

Because you are in a wheelchair, budget extra time. Honor your words and be on time!

## Lying and Idle Chatter

Unfortunately, the dating world is rife with lying and idle chatter. It's why some people dread dating and why many relationships fail. Breaking that pattern takes awareness, intention, and courage.

Many dating books endorse the practice of misleading dates. Who hasn't heard the benefits of playing hard to get? But misrepresenting your interest in your date to keep them interested is a terrible foundation for a healthy relationship.

For me, lying and idle chatter in dating were an ingrained pattern. I wanted to retain a sense of agency and power. When I told my date I'd call her later, I didn't have to face rejection in case she didn't want to make further plans. I could decide if I wanted to move forward—or not. I didn't see any harm in this. Now I realize that my words left my date confused, unsure of my intentions.

When you speak evasively, you're planting the seed to be treated the same way. Now both of you are hiding your true feelings, and the relationship has more obstacles because the trust between you is diminished.

My spiritual practice led me to reflect on the miscommunication that happened with Jordan in the lobby of my building. I recognized it as a form of idle chatter. And it wasn't an isolated incident: I had a habit of communicating with vagueness. "I'll call you" was what I said at the end of

 @patschang

all my dates, regardless of how I felt. It was easy and safe and gave me time to figure out my feelings. If I liked my date, I would call her. If I didn't, I would delay the call indefinitely, hoping she would get the hint.

"I'll call you" is perfectly polite and safe. It's also perfectly confusing and weak. I wasn't aware of this pattern of miscommunication—and it wasn't just in my dating life. I was saying "I'll call you" to family, friends, and colleagues, using it like "goodbye." I was protecting myself from being hurt by putting myself in a position of power.

I wanted to stop my confusing and weak speech, so I started to speak with a clear intention: I would tell my date, "Let's have dinner on Tuesday. Would seven o'clock work for you?"

People prefer concrete information. Think how confusing it is when you've had a great time together but don't hear from your date for days. If my date knows she'll have dinner with me on Tuesday, she doesn't spend Sunday and Monday doubting me.

## Practice on Friends

Communication skills are much easier to practice on friends.

Go through your contact list and call someone you haven't kept in touch with. Listen to that person with awareness, and provide the qualities you want in your date during the conversation.

End the conversation on a high note. Invite to catch up over a drink. Make concrete plans, and be on time.

## Intention

Speaking with awareness means knowing your intentions and being true to them. Most people mean well; they want a date to succeed. But their insecurities, or their ego, or the book they read on playing hard to get takes over. They end up saying something that doesn't match their true feelings. It causes hurt, confusion, and doubt.

Dating is stressful enough without having to guess what your partner intends to do next. You want a fun, engaged, and kind partner, not a chess opponent. Rehab your speech. Speak with clarity, and follow through. Let your date know she's going out with someone who honors his word.

While everyone benefits when we speak with awareness, not all people communicate in the same way. That's why it's so important to know the five different styles of communication and how to tailor your own communication to each one.

*Chapter 7*

# Get in the Comfort Zone

## Concert Cuddle

After Jordan, I started seeing Cara. After several dates, I still didn't feel a strong connection, and I wondered if she could see past the wheelchair. Dates at coffee shops and restaurants weren't helping our relationship progress. So I stepped outside my comfort zone and took her somewhere where *she* would feel comfortable.

When I overheard her talking excitedly on the phone about her favorite Chinese pop star coming to Beijing, I took a risk and bought concert tickets.

I had been to only a few concerts in my life, partly because of wheelchair accessibility. At many US concert venues, seats can be removed in certain sections to accommodate wheelchairs. In China, I didn't know what to expect.

At the venue, my fears were realized: steps everywhere, no wheelchair-accessible seating, no one to help me. I panicked that this inconvenience would turn Cara off. Thinking fast, I flagged down a staff member. He grabbed another person, and they lifted me up some stairs and into a seat. It was a regular concert seat, without a seatbelt, and I worried I might fall out if bumped by a passerby.

I was out of my element, but Cara was in hers, and I let that energy fill me. I joked to her that I wasn't stable in the chair, so we'd need to hold on to each other to keep me from falling. She laughed and hugged me, turning her arms into my seatbelt. It was the most affection we'd shared in our short relationship.

I was seated on the aisle, and when other people started filing into our row, they expected me to stand for them. I just shrugged and said I couldn't. Some of them got really irritated. Cara and I laughed about that too. It became our inside joke that I was the rudest audience member at the concert.

We hugged and laughed our way through that night at the arena. I don't even remember the music. The experience fast-forwarded our relationship, deepening our connection and boosting my confidence in her feelings toward me.

Buying those tickets took me out of my comfort zone, but it showed her I cared and wanted to share the things she enjoyed. And for Cara, an auditory experience helped her relax and open up.

As a quad, I am often outside of my comfort zone. It can feel like the world is made for the able-bodied, but the truth is that life is a give-and-take. No one can be in their element all the time. The same is true of dating. As you learn to meet each other outside of your personal comfort zones, you will find yourselves growing closer. Engaging with different faculties affords new worlds of adventure— physically, mentally, emotionally, and spiritually.

## Different Styles of Engagement

Getting into someone's comfort zone means finding out how they engage the world. These styles of engagement can be grouped into five categories: visual, verbal, tactile, auditory, and action. Once you figure out your date's preferred engagement style, you can tailor your outings to suit it.

For example, if your date is auditory, go to a concert. For a visual person, go to an art gallery. Take a tactile date to a pottery class, a verbal person to a coffeehouse, and an action-oriented person on a hike. Until I invited Cara to that auditory experience, I wasn't aware of the importance of this.

Getting to know someone in their preferred setting will help them relax and enjoy themselves more. When you ignore your date's engagement style, the relationship may quickly stall and fizzle. If I had kept repeating my usual dating routine, Cara might have thought I was cool but not someone she could connect with.

Comfortable at the concert, Cara was affectionate and playful. When you identify your date's comfort zone, you'll unlock a core part of their personality. It brings you closer.

 @patschang

Discovering your date's preferred style is often trial and error. Use your listening skills for clues. Go back to Chapter 5 for a refresher on listening.

Watching someone interact with others and their environment also provides clues. From my experiences, tactile people tend to enjoy eating with their hands and don't mind getting a little messy. They also love to hug and cuddle! Pay attention, and people's preferences will be revealed.

---

### Sing Your Heart Out

Getting comfortable means expressing your feelings without fear.

Here's a fun way to practice for those who don't usually sing or express themselves through singing.

Choose your favorite songs and sing them aloud in your car or shower. Better yet, sing at a karaoke! You don't have to choose a sappy love song. Try something different!

Be a good companion everywhere and to everyone. Feel with an open heart, and connect with love. This plants a seed for open and creative engagement.

---

## Give and Receive

Finding your date's comfort zone—and then acting on it—
is a form of giving. You're prioritizing *her* enjoyment, not
yours.

In a meditative practice called *give-and-take*, you visualize giving your happiness to others and taking on their suffering. It's the purest form of altruism and a speedy method
of cultivating compassion: you develop the recognition that
everyone is equal, everyone wants to be happy, and no one
wants to be unhappy. It's like putting yourself in someone
else's place, giving them happiness because you understand
their needs and wants.

In dating, we often go places and do things *we* enjoy. But
don't assume what works for you will work for others. This
assumption, if left unchecked, can weaken, or even end, a
relationship. When your date looks uncomfortable, bored,
or guarded, or she checks her phone too often, turn off that
self-cherishing behavior and change your approach.

If you have no clue about your date's engagement style
after a few dates, it could mean you haven't asked questions
mindfully or listened well. You might also be habitually distracted. Ask yourself: Am I present? How can I listen deeply?
What gets her excited? Then put yourself in her position, and
plan the ideal date.

Although this practice is meant to serve your date, it's
not entirely selfless. You'll reap the benefits, getting more

 @patschang

intimate with your partner and forming a more satisfying connection.

## How You Eat Reflects How You Date

"Really?!"

Yes, and I'm not talking about your table manners.

When you eat, do you watch TV? Read a book? Swipe your phone? Check out Instagram posts? Daydream?

I did. I thought I was multitasking and saving time. But it actually took longer to eat, and I wasn't fully appreciating the food or the show/book/dream.

I was eating without tasting. I was reading without comprehending.

This habit of distracted eating will distract you on your date. Even when you want to focus on your date and be present, you won't be. This is how powerful habits are.

Your date will certainly notice your mental absence.

By practicing mindful eating—that is, eating without the TV or your phone—you will be an aware and present date. Practicing mindfulness and concentration brings powerful connections.

@patschang

## Walk and Talk

When you're relaxed and spontaneous on dates, you can discover a date's engagement style serendipitously.

After dinner with one of my dates, Emma, my driver didn't show up. With Beijing's heavy traffic, it's not unusual for my driver to be late. The restaurant was located near a large pedestrian mall. Rather than sit and wait for our ride, we checked out the mall.

I rolled in my wheelchair, and Emma walked beside me as we window-shopped. I noticed that she was more talkative, upbeat, and engaged than she had been at dinner. She began walking in circles around my chair, pointing things out and laughing. A light bulb went on: Emma was an action person. Being able to communicate as she moved made her more comfortable.

We had a great time strolling the mall. When we finally returned to the restaurant, I leaned over and kissed her on the lips. That night was a turning point in our relationship. We went from a couple of meandering dates to developing a real romance.

## Shopping Connection

We aren't limited to one style of engagement. Some people feel comfortable with any style, while others have an equal preference for two or three out of the five.

 @patschang

On Antonia's first day in San Francisco, when she visited me for the first time, she was jet-lagged and quiet. I couldn't read how she was feeling about me. I sensed she was a tactile communicator because she always dropped down on her knees and gave me a big hug when we greeted each other. On our walk to the restaurant, Antonia didn't talk. I took her hand and smiled at her, and she smiled back. Even though we said nothing, I felt our connection.

Our table wasn't ready, so we went into a nearby housewares store. I normally avoid going into stores, as it's awkward to navigate the aisles in my ponderous electric wheelchair. But I knew I should push out of my comfort zone.

Antonia loved examining the kitchenware. She still didn't talk much, but she picked up an oddly shaped oven mitt and put it on me, and she showed me some cool appliances. Her face lit up, and she was like a kid in a toy shop! I realized that Antonia liked both *doing* and *touching*: action and tactile. She really came alive in that store, and the spark she gave off ignited our relationship and brought us closer.

## Win-Win

It's important to plan dates that suit the engagement style of both you and your date. In the same way that your date will be off if they're out of their comfort zone, you will be too. As you might have guessed already, I'm a verbal person (Too verbal, some would say!). In a way, that's the easiest comfort zone style to accommodate. I can talk wherever, whenever. My challenge was figuring out what, in addition to talking, would make my dates happy and comfortable.

Sure, I don't particularly enjoy listening to concerts. I can't easily go on a bike ride or hike in the woods. I can't do much with my hands. The key is that I was present.

Don't let your disability dictate your dating activities. That's another way of limiting yourself. The best dates include give-and-take, a way for each of you to spend some time in your preferred comfort zone. Maybe that means starting on a walk and ending at dinner, or listening to a concert and then getting coffee.

In the next chapter, we look at the next step of getting comfortable: being honest. Expressing your feelings, both positive and negative, will give your relationship room to grow.

*Chapter 8*

# Honestly, Do You Wear a Diaper?

## Bad at Breakups

I hate being the bad guy. I'm the smart guy, the thoughtful guy, the charming guy (or so I hope). But I learned the hard way that being the honest guy is the only path forward.

I once dated a woman named Kate, a buxom event organizer. After six months, she began seeking a bigger commitment, even mentioning marriage. I wasn't ready. I wanted to have fun and meet lots of people. I enjoyed her company, but I wanted our relationship to stay casual.

Did I tell her the truth? No way. I thought that sharing my honest feelings would let her down, and I'd be taking on the bad-guy role I so carefully avoided. So when she continued to seek commitment, I did the lame guy thing—I pulled back.

I returned fewer of her calls and asked her out less often. I deluded myself into thinking this a kinder way to let her down. As you might expect, she didn't agree. She saw my behavior for what it was: cowardly, dishonest, and disrespectful.

 @patschang

My intentions were good, but I ended up doing exactly what I was trying to avoid. I became the bad guy. My dishonesty led to a really ugly breakup.

Honesty comes from actions, not just words. If you're dishonest about where the relationship is going, you'll eventually have to choose—be honest or take the cowardly path and hurt both of you. My best adventures have happened when I've had the courage to be honest.

## Phone Call Fail

Being honest with your date can be as simple as voicing your communication preference. Maybe you need alone time, but your date likes constant company. Being open about this difference helps you date in a mutually satisfying way.

Candace, a woman I dated, liked me to call her every day. I didn't love talking every day but kept that feeling to myself, not wanting to offend her. To appease her, I called at the same time—four o'clock—every afternoon. Later, she told me my punctuality irritated her. *Screw this*, I thought. *This girl is impossible to please.* Instead of discussing it with her, I called her less frequently. It worked.

We eventually stopped dating.

Candace probably noticed I treated our phone calls like homework. I was going through the motions, checking that appointment off my schedule, when really, I'd have preferred seeing her a few nights a week. Just as with Kate, I withheld my true feelings and intentions, and it ended badly.

 @patschang

I still wonder what would have happened if I had told Candace that I loved seeing her a couple nights a week and that I was not ready to commit more. She might have been fine with that, and I could have gotten exactly the relationship I wanted at that stage in my life. But because I wasn't honest, I lost the opportunity.

Of course, not everything should be revealed on a first date, or even a third or fourth. But as long as you don't actively conceal key parts of yourself, your relationship will grow from a strong foundation. Be honesty from the beginning.

---

### One of the Best Gifts

Honesty is one of the most extravagant gifts you can give a date.

But first, give it to yourself. Here's one way.

First thing in the morning, write and recite the following:

I will speak with truthfulness for the next hour.

Then be honest for one hour. Don't expect it to be easy! But remember: many small successes lead to a spectacular life.

Plant a seed for honesty.

---

## Honest, Not Brutal

Sometimes, honesty can be brutal. That's not the kind of honesty I'm advocating. I would never tell a date I don't find her attractive because of her big nose. Similarly, I wouldn't want someone to tell me that they could never date someone in a wheelchair.

The kind of honesty I'm talking about comes from a place of respect and authenticity. You owe it to yourself and your date to be honest about yourself and your feelings. Yes, you want to put your best foot forward, but you shouldn't misrepresent yourself. That only sets you both up for misery.

## Leg Bag Emergency

If you're disabled, you may be extra reluctant to reveal your true self to a date. Maybe you have conditions that frustrate or embarrass you, and you're convinced these things will turn off a potential romantic partner.

For years I struggled to present myself directly and honestly. I can't hide my wheelchair, of course, but I wanted to counteract that image by giving an impression of independence and strength. I went to great lengths to hide my vulnerability from my dates. I even kept myself dehydrated to avoid emptying my leg bag. That leg bag was always my last major obstacle to intimacy with a woman.

 @patschang

*Will she want to sleep with me after she sees this leg bag?* I deliberated.

I knew I wanted to date Antonia because of her beauty and cheerful personality. However, I had doubts about a long-term relationship. *Can a girl this beautiful and fun be marriage material? Probably not. Marriage is serious. Solemn. I will just have fun with her.*

I kept this thought from Antonia. I crossed my fingers as her visit to San Francisco approached. *Please don't screw this up, Pat.* Days before her first flight to San Francisco, when we were on the phone finalizing travel details, she asked me an unexpected question: "Pat, do you wear diapers?"

My worst fear had come true.

My heart pounded and I became lightheaded. The fun, intimate plans I had for the visit crumbled. *If I tell her the truth, she'll cancel the trip. If I lie to her, she'll find out when she's here, which is worse.*

My mind raced through what seemed like hundreds of possible outcomes. I blurted out, "I don't wear diapers." As nonchalantly as possible, I added, "I use a leg bag, so I can pee when public bathrooms aren't accessible. Why do you ask?"

"My mum and I took care of my father the last six months of his life," she said. "He lost control of his bowel and bladder and wore diapers. I wanted to know your routine."

Antonia's answer surprised me. Her openness and sincerity took my breath away. There I was, planning the trip with pleasure and little else in mind, while Antonia's motivation was getting to know me. To her, my paralysis wasn't an obstacle or a turn-off. She was honest without being insensitive.

Her love and affection for me, someone she barely knew, was so real and transparent that my feeling toward her shifted instantly. *This is not a typical girl,* I thought. *She could be the one for me.*

When we had been married a few months, we met my parents for lunch at a shopping mall in Beijing. As Antonia pushed me toward the restaurant, I felt myself peeing. I looked down and saw a dark spot growing between my legs.

"Shit!" I cursed and told Antonia we needed to find a bathroom quickly. Hearing the panic in my voice, she sprinted toward the bathroom, her flowy dress flying out behind her. The way Antonia pushed that wheelchair, you'd think we were being chased by an angry mob.

We found that the tube to my leg bag was kinked. We straightened it and cleaned up my pants as best we could. Antonia laughed, thinking of how we'd raced to the bathroom for what she considered a pretty minor problem.

I felt very self-conscious, certain that everyone would stare and realize I had peed in my pants. To my surprise, no one even glanced at me. At the restaurant, my parents had no idea I had been soaked in urine. No one noticed, except me.

At first, the incident felt like a nightmare. The thing I tried to hide at all costs had a very public malfunction. But in the end, it really wasn't a big deal. Antonia didn't care. And when we did sit down at the restaurant, my parents didn't even notice.

It mattered only to me.

I now know that my leg bag is something I can be honest about. I need it to pee, and sometimes it can leak. Just like my leg bag, the truth of your disability isn't so terrible that other people can't handle it. Be honest with your date.

## Be Honest with Yourself

You can't be honest with your date unless you're first honest with yourself. I had to admit that my leg bag was a necessary part of my life, not something terrible. Only then could I feel comfortable showing it to other people.

"The truth will set you free" is a cliché, but it's an appropriate description of how honesty gives you the freedom to be yourself with others. Presenting your truth to the world puts you more at ease.

Being at ease on a date conveys confidence. When we're comfortable enough to be honest about ourselves, our feelings, and our intentions, we have better dates. We also set ourselves up for better long-term relationships. When I wanted to appear confident, I practiced how to hold my drink and dress well; I dominated conversations. Real confidence, however, comes from being transparent. Why would you be nervous when you have nothing to hide?

*Chapter 9*

# Ramp Up Generosity

## Big Tipper

Back in New York, my friend Homan and I took a taxi ride together. Although the taxi had a ramp and was wheelchair accessible, the cab driver didn't know how to fasten the tie-downs to secure my wheelchair. Worse yet, he got lost on the way to our destination. When we got out, Homan handed him a surprisingly generous tip, over 25 percent of the fare.

"Why such a big tip?" I understood rewarding for great service, but this driver didn't qualify.

"This is how he makes his living," Homan said.

"Exactly. It's his job. He didn't provide good service, so he doesn't deserve a big tip."

"He's committed his precious life to provide a valuable service. We should be grateful."

Homan's attitude silenced me. A friend since junior high, he's accomplished and hardworking, but the quality that makes him special is generosity. Early on, I noticed he was generous with family and friends. It took a few decades of friendship to discover he's generous with everyone. By

@patschang

ramping up his generosity, he had created beautiful relationships and an amazing life.

## A Giving Mindset

Generous people don't see life as a balance sheet of credits and debits. They don't think the cab driver needs to go above and beyond to get a big tip. They share their wealth without condition or calculation. In my experience, generous people are happier.

Many of us bring to dating a very different mindset. We worry that giving too much makes us seem desperate or opens us up to exploitation. Some of us think it's unfair to give more than we get, and in a good relationship, each person should give an equal amount.

That unspoken scorekeeping prevents us from getting close. Our interactions feel like transactions rather than two people forming a connection. The calculating that sometimes happens on a date is counterproductive to success. It gives off the wrong energy, and it complicates matters. When you adopt a generous mindset instead, your dating experience can be more joyful.

If you have a disability, you could be used to receiving. You may wonder what you have to give. I want to be clear that generosity means giving with the understanding that reciprocity will happen, often in surprising ways, and *what* and *how much* you give are up to you. You can be generous with your possessions, your time, your skills, your heart, or your money. Giving more doesn't necessarily mean the same thing for every person: if you have a busy schedule, fifteen minutes of your time is generous. If your calendar is empty, an hour might mean nothing.

Because you don't know others' circumstances and motivation, avoid judging how generous they are. When someone is generous, rejoice over their kindness.

Like many things in life, generosity comes back to you. When you give generously, the world often finds a way to repay you extravagantly. Give without expectation, but trust that you'll receive something back. You can't predict the timing or packaging, but know it will come. Knowing this, you will find it easier to be generous.

## Small Fun

This small exercise in generosity adds up quickly.

Every day, put two dollars in an envelope. This is *fun* money!

In a year, you'll have $730 for fun activities.

Plant a seed for a consistently fun attitude.

## The Dating Game

Knowing how much to give was tricky for me. I often took dates to fancy, trendy restaurants. But not out of generosity.

I wanted to impress them with my exquisite taste and deep pockets. Yet I also worried about spending too much: Would women think I was loaded? Would they think I went overboard, trying too hard because I got only one date a year? Every action I took could be interpreted in multiple ways.

I also wondered what to expect in return. Does one fancy dinner equal one goodnight kiss? Does a week of expensive dates equal coming up to my apartment? If nothing happens, is she taking advantage of me? Men, I admit, are usually the worst calculators. I fell victim to this in a serious way. I expected to receive repayment in the form of physical affection. I kept a running tab in my head of what I'd invested—and what I hoped to receive in return.

But what happens if each person has her own point system? For you, buying two sought-after concert tickets might repay the three dinners your date has paid for. In her mind, you might owe the concert *and* dessert *and* coming back to her place. If each person has a different point system, keeping a score isn't possible. It can only complicate a relationship.

And when you're calculating scores, it's tough to be relaxed and engaged. You notice she orders the lobster and make a mental note when she gets dessert, and then you bang your head against the wall when she doesn't hold your hand.

Don't assume your date doesn't notice you're keeping score. You're probably not being as subtle as you think. Eventually, your calculating mindset will lead to frustration, even anger. The rules of this game aren't clear to both players. For all you know, your dates might not even know they're playing a game.

If you instead adopt a spirit of generosity—giving with the understanding that you will receive something back, but that reciprocity will happen in surprising ways—you take pressure off both of you. You set yourself up for happier dates and more possibilities. Generosity ramps up your dating life.

## Be My Guest

Another fun way to practice generosity is to invite friends over for meals.

Start with simple brunches on weekends, and gradually work your way up to dinner parties.

As you develop more experience, experiment with more creative and elaborate arrangements. You can use your fun money for these events.

Consistency is key.

As a wheelchair user, I used to believe I couldn't entertain. *How am I supposed to cook? How can I set the table? How do I serve food?*

@patschang

Many guys, not just guys in wheelchairs, don't know how to cook, set the table, or serve.

We can all learn, however, and, with practice, become good at anything, including cooking, setting the table, or serving. I didn't think my brother, Jeff, could even learn how to boil water to make instant noodles. His signature dish was pepperoni and mushroom pizza, piping hot from Domino's. When he and I were roommates, we didn't need to set the table because there was no dining table!

Then Jeff surprised everyone by enrolling in culinary school and completing a degree in culinary arts. Although he did not pursue a career in the restaurant industry, he uses those cooking skills every day to the benefit of his family and friends.

If your disability is so severe that you can't perform any of these tasks, enlist a friend or family member to help. You can also order takeout and present the food thoughtfully, even with paper plates and disposable utensils. You are far more capable and resourceful than you believe.

Entertaining friends develops your leadership and organizing ability, two highly attractive skills. Invite your date to your dinner party!

## Generous Spirit

My dates took on new energy once I understood generosity is a way of life. If I bought concert tickets or planned a trip, it wasn't because I was desperate to impress a woman, but because I felt we both would enjoy the experience.

If you don't have a lot of money, offer to go Dutch or make dinner at home. The idea is to act in the spirit of generosity in whatever way that you can. Maybe your date insists on always paying for dinner. Accept her generosity graciously. You can show yours by helping her create a cool app, buying tickets to a show, or booking a hotel over the weekend as a surprise. Be creative. You can be generous with your time, skills, talents, and connections.

By acting generously, you build up goodwill among the people around you. If you've shown others generosity, it's far more likely they'll be generous in return. When you apply that to dating, you'll build a relationship with someone in the spirit of giving. What a wonderful tone to set as the foundation.

I didn't enter my relationship with Antonia with this mindset, and I was lucky that she's a naturally generous person. She still teaches me lessons about generosity.

One day, we passed a street sweeper on our walk. Antonia smiled and said hello in her joyful way. When I remarked on this, she came back with a question: "What does a smile cost?"

"Nothing. It's free."

"So why not give it freely?" she said.

If you can't even give away what's free, how can you learn to give away things that you value? If love is your most valuable possession, how can you give it away when you can't part with a smile?

Generosity is a skill. The more we perform acts of generosity, the more natural it becomes. The way you choose to be generous reflects your unique personality and abilities. Practice often, and it will change your world in positive ways beyond your imagination.

## Share the Pleasure

For the next week, stop giving yourself pleasure. Stop masturbating.

And, if you haven't already, stop watching porn.

*What the . . . ?* You're thinking.

After all, the doctors never said masturbating is bad for you! It feels good! It's free! It's harmless!

Think about it this way: If you have a spinal cord injury and no sensation below your level of injury, why are you stroking it when you can't feel it?

Even if you *can* feel it (and love stroking it), redirect that energy! Work on things to improve your dating life (e.g., the exercises in this book).

> Don't be selfish. Give someone else the pleasure of giving you pleasure. Let your date experience the joy of stroking you.
>
> Stop stroking yourself, and you will get stroked!

## The Little Things

With a disability, sometimes it's a struggle to think of something you can offer that someone else can't do just as well— or better. For me, I can't open the door for my dates, carry them over puddles, or open stuck jar lids.

But I found other ways to affirm my dates. I made them laugh, kept them entertained, listened closely, and planned outings they would enjoy.

Receiving graciously is also a form of giving. When your date (or anyone) offers you a drink or a helping hand, accept with a smile and appreciation. By receiving, you are allowing others to become better at giving!

Being generous made me a much better companion, and it greatly improved the quality of my relationships. Once I stopped keeping score, it became so much easier to score!

*Chapter 10*

# No Quickie in Celebration

## Dark Vision

The water in the pool glistened like lapis lazuli. The clean scent of falling rain competed with the smell of chlorine. Swim goggles in hand, I walked along the poolside, eager to start practice.

Thirteen and muscular, I was one of the hard-core swimmers; only a select few had shown up today. I loved practices like this because I got extra time with the coach to perfect my skills.

My starting dive needed improvement. Coach said I was entering the water too soon. Standing at the edge of the starting block, I felt on top of the world. Fit and physically attractive, I owned the pool, I owned my classes, and girls loved me.

Each time I dove, I made small adjustments so my head would hit the water at the perfect angle. I'd listen to my coach's feedback, then hop back up on the block to try again.

For one particular dive, I hesitated for a split second before I leaped off the block, stretching my neck awkwardly before

@patschang

bending toward the water. The second my head entered the pool, my vision went dark for what felt like a long blink. Suddenly, the water was bright again. I could see someone's arm near me. *Whoa, someone's in my lane*, I thought. *That's really dangerous.*

With my next blink, I realized it was my own arm. I floated face down, unable to move. My arms, legs, and torso seemed completely disconnected from my brain.

I sensed pressure around my body as someone dragged me to the pool edge and turned my face up. My coach stared down at me, his brow furrowed.

"Keep your head steady," he said, holding my head with both hands. I stared at the gray sky through fogged-up goggles. Drizzle spattered my face and goggles. I felt calm.

Soon the paramedics arrived. They lifted me out of the pool and onto a gurney. In the ambulance, one paramedic held my head to prevent my neck from turning. My body began to feel cold, and I drifted to sleep.

At the hospital, doctors ran a bunch of tests. They found no visible signs of trauma to my head and no marks on my hands. They said my neck must have bent too far forward and broken on contact with the water. A freak accident.

A few days after the accident, my father came into the hospital room to tell me I would be in a wheelchair for the rest of my life. My world collapsed. My life was over.

The only reason I didn't give up right then was because I didn't know how to.

For the next few weeks, I let reality sink in. I told myself I would not let the injury defeat me and rob me of a good life. I would fight.

## The Fight

*Pat, you are a fighter!*
*You will win the battle!*
*You will overcome adversity!*
*You are a wheelchair warrior!*

These mantras fueled me. I persevered. I fought. I overcame obstacles, hardships, and long odds.

I told myself, multiple times daily, that pushing myself reflected how I felt about being disabled: life in a wheelchair is a fight, a struggle, an adversity.

I kept using these words, and unconsciously I started to believe that life *is* a fight, a struggle, an adversity. Nothing would come without a battle.

If you're reading this book, you're already an expert at persevering. You've overcome hardships, obstacles, and long odds. You've got determination and grit. But do you remember to celebrate that?

Like me, you might also feel that other aspects of life, especially dating, is a fight, a struggle. With this attitude, I couldn't feel joy from my successes. How could I, when life is "a fight, a struggle, an adversity"? How could I appreciate life when it's "a fight, a struggle, an adversity"?

@patschang

No wonder my relationships failed! I turned loving, fun, sexy dates into obstacles, struggles, adversaries, and enemies!

We seldom celebrate our successes. When we don't, we're just grinding, suffering, and pushing ourselves through the bitterness. When we consciously celebrate each milestone, we feel rejuvenated. We have the energy to keep going.

I used to wonder why relationship celebrations—First date anniversary, Valentine's Day, wedding anniversaries, etc.—were necessary. Can't we just celebrate everything together once a year? Buying flowers each time was a waste. They just die. Can't we get a BBQ grill instead?

Now I understand the importance of such celebrations. Without them, we would never honor our relationship successes. Now I realize that every day is a celebration.

## Redefine Your Outcome

Little setbacks, like rejections, can derail you. What if we could eliminate setbacks and embrace what we have?

We can.

We can redefine a successful outcome: instead of *getting* a date, simply *asking* for a date can be the new goal. No matter what she says, as long as you take action, you will achieve success.

What are some other great outcomes? Improving yourself as a companion? Having fun? Bringing joy to other people?

 @patschang

Let's say a prospective partner doesn't call you after three really fun dates. If the outcome you defined was to have fun with your date—mission accomplished!

When you define a successful outcome this way, all progress is worth celebrating. You will approach dating with joyful perseverance and greatly increased your chances of happiness and success.

## Turn Bitter into Sweet

In Chinese, the word *ku* means bitterness. It also forms the term for *effort*, which literally translates to "pungent and bitter." Because of this, I used to believe that effort had to be paired with angst of some sort. No progress could be made without hardship: to accomplish anything, I must suffer. I instinctively reacted to many challenges with *ku*. When I was rejected by a date, feelings of *ku* engulfed me.

Another Chinese term, *jing jin*, means to continuously improve. Usually, this phrase is used to describe someone practicing something like martial arts until it becomes second nature. The challenge might be great, but persistence brings improvement. Perfect is a process, not a result.

I think of *jing jin* as an approach to dating that helps you avoid *ku*. If you let bitterness in, it will drain you of energy and joy on your dating journey. Gone will be the excitement of a new date, the pleasure of finding things in

 @patschang

common with someone, the thrill of a physical connection. When you are ruled by *ku*, it all becomes a chore. But when you embrace *jing jin*, you see dating as a series of constant improvements, each one worthy of celebration.

At one point in my life, dating became stale. After four or five dates, if I hadn't gotten what I wanted out of a relationship, I pulled back. I didn't realize that, in the spirit of *jing jin*, I should push forward.

Many people hit a plateau in dating. You've gone on several dates and gotten to know each other a little, but things stall. Your attitude is critical here. Are you going to be bitter, retreating to your single status, and stewing about your relationship woes? Or are you going to be like a world-class musician, honing your craft and breaking through to the next level?

The same philosophy applies to your dating life as a whole. Just because the last two people you dated were disasters, don't lose hope that the next one will be great.

---

### Bitterness to Sweetness

How can you turn bitterness into sweetness? Here's an exercise.

1. Write a list of your typical dating complaints:

- She hasn't texted me back.

---

 @patschang

- She must not like me.

- Dating sucks.

2. Rephrase with a positive spin:

- She hasn't called me back. This gives me more time to tidy up my place and try a new recipe for the dinner party.

- So many other women like me.

- Dating gives me more courage.

Everything has at least two sides. Be aware of what triggers negativity in you, and practice turning it into positivity.

## Celebrate Much and Often

One morning when I woke up, Antonia was hovering over me, grinning. "Get dressed! We're going out!"

"Where are we going?" I mumbled, wishing I could stay in bed.

"Just get ready! Quickly! We're celebrating!"

*Celebrating?*

Antonia's last-minute planning annoyed me, but when we pulled into McDonald's, my mood improved. *Cool! I hadn't had breakfast at McDonald's in years! Maybe she's craving hash browns?*

@patschang

The restaurant was surprisingly packed. I wheeled myself to one of the few available tables and waited for Antonia. She returned, beaming, with a tray of goodies, and yelled, "Happy Anniversary!"

Our fourth anniversary! And I hadn't remembered!

I tried not to act surprised—and tried even harder to hold back my tears. I'd always believed that only monumental achievements should be celebrated. *Why should I waste time and money celebrating minor accomplishments?* Yes, I even considered wedding anniversaries to be minor accomplishments. After all, we were already married, and no effort was required. What's there to celebrate?

That almost-forgotten wedding anniversary and an impromptu trip to McDonald's helped me understand that celebrating is a skill, one that requires mindful, consistent practice to hone. Celebrating motivates us and helps us to persist with joy.

Celebrate much and often, and your persevering will become joyous!

## Perseverance Leads to Joy

Joyful perseverance requires awareness and practice. You can transform life's blows into celebrations, stay motivated, and maximize your joy by redefining a successful outcome and striving for progress instead of results. Take every opportunity to celebrate, and don't forget that even small achievements are achievements.

When you learn to have joy, you begin to see so much you are grateful for and how important it is to appreciate the good *and* the bad things in your life.

*Chapter 11*

# Appreciation Therapy

## The Greatest Showman

After dating a while, I had gotten good at wooing women. But I hadn't mastered the art of follow-through.

*How much longer do I need to lie here?*

*My arm is getting numb.*

*How is the stock market doing?*

*Is it rude to wake her?*

"Hey. Are you hungry? Let's go get something to eat," I said, as softly and gently as I could.

"I want to stay in bed and cuddle some more . . . " she said sleepily, pulling her face closer to

mine and hugging me tighter.

*But you said that 21 minutes ago!*

I was a showman. A good one. Dating was my stage. I loved pursuing my date, impressing her, getting her to fall for me fast and hard.

After all, nothing comes close to the thrill of the chase.

But after I got what I wanted, the excitement began to fade. Even after a perfect date, I wanted to teleport myself

 @patschang

home. I couldn't wait to leave. If I stuck around, I would feel bored, even resentful. *Why am I doing all the work? I'm now her chef, concierge, lover, career counselor, and therapist! And she's living with me!*

I rarely thought about appreciating the person who was spending time with me. Even rarer did I say thank you. *Why should I? I'm the performer. I should be the one getting the thanks!*

I was expecting applause, accolades, and appreciation. But I wasn't giving them.

I mastered dating. I could get girls to fall for me. But I didn't want to be the fun guy who isn't marriage material, nor did I want to be the eager-to-please nice guy who finishes single. I was floundering because I couldn't see how important appreciation was.

Appreciation is the ultimate expression of receiving. When you appreciate the people in your life, a sense of abundance and fulfillment follows you everywhere. It's one of most important lessons I learned from dating. I call it appreciation therapy.

## Texts So Awesome She Can't Ignore

"hey hot stuff! quit thinking about me and focus on driving"

"haha you wish I am thinking about you"

 @patschang

"take off those wedges! you can't drive wearing cheesecakes"

After having an awesome time, I would text my date and thank her without saying thanks and tease her about her goofy shoes. She would text something cute back and subtly suggest we meet again. Soon.

My text wasn't sent out of genuine appreciation. It was effective flirting.

Appreciation didn't come naturally to me. Although I never verbalized it, my frequent thought was this: I'm already in a wheelchair. The world owes *me*.

Why would *I* appreciate?

Then I read about the world's greatest car salesperson, Joe Girard.

Joe sold over thirteen thousand cars during his fifteen-year career, earning a Guinness World Record. His trick to achieve this amazing feat? He handwrote thank you cards to his customers every month! And the content was unexpectedly simple: "I like you."

This technique sounded so simple and effective that I decided to try it. But after two weeks of writing thank you messages daily, I stopped. I couldn't come up with more people to appreciate! Through this attempt, I learned that appreciation is like a muscle. I knew it could be strengthened with training, but I wasn't sure how to go about doing that.

I needed to identify an exercise I could do daily.

Then a friend suggested that every day I write down 20 things I appreciate. These could include anyone and anything, simple or significant. And I could write in my journal and not send notes. The more I practiced, the more I recognized how great my life is: the wonderful people, places, things, and events I experience every day.

## Flowers for No Reason

Plant a seed for a mindset of appreciation.

Get a bouquet of fresh flowers for no reason and set it on the kitchen countertop or desk of someone important to you: A colleague? A relative? A date? Watch the reaction.

## Appreciate Supermodels Who Can't Fix Cars

Deliberately practicing appreciation unexpectedly helped me recognize there are no absolutes. There's good in the bad, and vice versa. But what about my wheelchair, the bane of my existence?

My wheelchair was my enemy. I believed for decades that all the setbacks in my life, especially in dating, resulted from being in a wheelchair. My wheelchair made dating extremely difficult. I couldn't see any good in my chair. Without it, I would have been dating supermodels. With it, I struggled!

 @patschang

It was easy to blame the wheelchair. It couldn't talk back. It couldn't tell me there might be other reasons I wasn't dating supermodels. It couldn't point out that I had an atomic temper and spoke harshly.

I refused to admit that without my wheelchair, I couldn't leave my house—to go on a date or otherwise. My wheelchair faithfully got me where I needed to go. It never had a sick day or took time off. It went on dates with me and waited patiently. It supported me through good times and bad times.

I didn't ever thank it or say "good job." Not once.

My focus was on the bad or, when my mood was good, on the "could be better." I couldn't see how wonderful my wheelchair was. When it needed repairs, I complained about the inconvenience and the cost. It was like dating a supermodel and complaining that she didn't know how to fix the retractable ramp of my modified van, then expecting her to stick around when I didn't appreciate her.

My wheelchair didn't leave me when I failed to appreciate it.

What about the women I dated? I appreciated them, initially. The first few dates were intoxicating. *Her beauty! Her wit! Her charm!* Then the faults emerged: Rachel talked too much. Monica talked too little. Phoebe was too loud. Even the venues started to annoy me. *This dive bar is too rowdy. That bar isn't happening enough. This Indian restaurant's chicken tikka is too spicy; that one's isn't spicy enough.*

My relationships fizzled because I lost appreciation when everything became routine. Yet when breakups ensued, I felt dejected and resentful. It didn't make sense: If I didn't want a relationship, shouldn't breaking up be a good thing? But I didn't know what I wanted or how to appreciate what I had.

## Score through Appreciation

1. If you don't love yourself, who's going to love you?

   Look into the mirror and say, "I'm thankful that you're here."

   Plant a seed to produce endless love.

2. 20 = score!

   Write down 20 things/people/events/places you appreciate. If it's hard, start with three and gradually increase. Review the list weekly and observe patterns. What do you appreciate? If those items keep repeating, develop an appreciation for new things.

3. End on a high note

   Now that you have surprised your date with flowers (Flowers for No Reason exercise, Chapter 11), you can take it to the next level.

> Do you typically present flowers at the beginning of the date? Your date will be tickled if you unexpectedly show appreciation at the *end* of the date! Plan where to hide flowers so you can pull them out with great fanfare when saying goodbye, and watch her delight.
>
> It will make a different impression. You will score.

## Appreciate the Bad

Look closely, and you will see that nothing is fully "bad." Without the unsuccessful dates, I wouldn't have become a better date. Without rejections, I would never have become the person Antonia was interested in. My dates and relationships, which caused me so much heartache and angst, were my best teacher.

Without my accident and spinal cord injury, which I perceived as "bad," Antonia would not be in my life today.

Appreciate the relationships you've had. They aren't failures. They're not disasters. They helped you grow. They got you here. And those experiences will help you reach the goal—whatever it may be—that makes you appreciate every moment of your life.

*Chapter 12*

# Karma Sutra

## How to Create Luck

"You are so lucky, Pat! Antonia is wonderful!"

I hear this a lot. And she is. Throughout our marriage, I have often reflected on my good fortune.

Until one day, I realized that it wasn't luck. It can't be. The amount of luck required for me to randomly meet my perfect companion is so huge that it requires a miracle.

It was not by chance. Somehow I created luck. But how?

I retraced my relationship with Antonia and simplified it to the most crucial components: when and where we met, and who introduced us.

- I met Antonia through my friend Steven.

- I met Steven in Beijing.

- I was in Beijing because my parents were in Beijing.

If I were not good friends with Steven, he would not have invited me to the Peking duck dinner, when I met Antonia

 @patschang

for the first time, or asked me to be the best man at his wedding, when I met Antonia for the second time.

I was a good companion to Steven.

I would not have met Steven without being in Beijing. And I was in Beijing because my parents encouraged me to explore opportunities in Asia. They helped me settle in Beijing, and we were able to spend a lot more time together.

I was a good companion to my parents.

By being a good companion to my friend and parents, I created the conditions for me to meet Antonia! I created more than luck. I created a miracle.

The companionship I provided led me to my perfect companion.

Be a good companion, and you will have good companionship.

Be a good companion to all, and you will have amazing companionship.

## Seeds of Relationships

The surface of the swimming pool glistened, mirrorlike. I sat tensely in my wheelchair, watching the water. After rehab, I had vowed never to return to a swimming pool. Now, 29 years later, I sat facing my deepest fear.

But this time, I was surrounded by close friends and the greatest love of my life, Antonia.

The pool at our condo was calm and quiet, the sound of children's voices far away. As Antonia removed my shirt, I inhaled the warm, moist air.

During the past three years, in an effort to start a family, we had gone through four IVF (in vitro fertilization) procedures but failed to conceive. Each time, our hopes would soar, only to crash. We felt frustrated and puzzled. Why were we having so much trouble?

"Unexplained infertility," we were told. Modern medicine should have worked—but didn't. Both Antonia and I were healthy, and we followed the protocol exactly.

Then our spiritual teacher suggested I imagine myself as a father: "Do what fathers do, and you will become a father."

The first image that came to mind was my yet-to-be-born children laughing and splashing in a swimming pool with Antonia and me. Painful as it was, I needed to return to the pool.

I was ready. My friends Ein and Ian lifted me from the wheelchair—one hugging me from behind and one holding my knees—and shuffled down the steps of the pool. Another friend, already in the pool, supported my waist and inched me into the water. As my body entered the water, it stiffened, triggering a muscle spasm.

I floated on my back and breathed slowly. Soon my body relaxed, and the muscle spasm subsided. I was ready to go further.

"Let me submerge my head," I said.

I held my breath as my friends turned me upright and cautiously lowered me. My ears submerged, and the world went silent. No human sounds, just the eerie white noise of the pulsating pool. Panic shot up my chest. My body struggled vigorously.

I could no longer hold my breath. Fear gripped me, and I thrashed my arms.

Then, in the watery void, an angelic face appeared: Antonia looked into my eyes and gave me a gentle, reassuring smile.

The fear subsided, and I held my breath for a few more seconds before coming up for air. Feeling calmer, I noticed I could float and control my body well.

For the first time in 29 years, I was swimming again.

Nine months later, Antonia was pregnant. She gave birth to our beautiful son, and I look forward to teaching him to swim.

That day I learned that my reproductive life wasn't separate from the rest of my life. The same is true of your dating. Your dating life bears the fruit of everything you think and do. When you plant seeds for companionship, your life blossoms with its fruits. What you do in your life affects your dating life.

This is cause and effect: what you put out comes back to you. What you sow, you reap. The ancient sutras—spiritual texts—say this. It's the law of the universe. And it's what I call "karma sutra."

## Relationship Sutras

Every lesson I've shared with you in this book is about uplifting your mind—living head over wheels. You can gain a fresh start by cleaning up your clutter and letting go of judgment and past trauma. You can elevate your romance by listening and communicating with mindfulness. And you can enhance your relationships by being honest, generous, joyfully persistent, and appreciative. Each positive change takes you closer to the relationship of your dreams.

Looking back, I can see how every fear, frustration, and embarrassment I experienced during my dating adventures taught me lessons about becoming a loving companion. After facing my worst fear in the pool, I began swimming regularly and now can swim without assistance. Envisioning my healthy, vibrant children, I released more painful memories. As I plant the seeds for my future, I look forward to reaping the benefits of more loving relationships.

## Blank Slate

We sometimes think our actions and thoughts don't matter because the world seems so vast. What can one person do?

But every action and thought matters. If you persistently direct them toward the path you want to take, your world will change in that direction. This is the deepest, most profound truth. Your dating life starts out as a blank slate of possibilities. It's intrinsically empty. The actions and thoughts you put into your dates shape your dating life. The principles are simple:

- If you want joy, bring joy to yourself and others.

- If you want kindness, be kind to yourself and others.

- If you want love, love yourself and others.

I learned these universal principles through Buddhist teachings, but they are the foundation of other spiritual traditions.

I used to think about the world in a probabilistic sense—things happen by chance. Now I know that's not true. I've seen firsthand how my life has changed as I began to tend it mindfully.

I could never have built such a beautiful, fulfilling relationship with Antonia without applying these principles. My married life is everything I imagined and more, fulfilling and joyous. And I would not have embarked on this journey without these lessons. If you take only one thing from this book, it should be this: we create our own reality, which is limitless if we do not set limits on it.

## Empty Box

Antonia pushed my chair quickly. "The solemnization ceremony is about to start," she said. "Let's get closer so we can hear!"

It was my first time attending a wedding in Singapore, and I didn't know what to expect. The bride and groom stood in front of our spiritual teacher, Lama, who gave them a box. "Please open it," he said, smiling.

The bride and groom opened the lid and stared. *What's in it?* I wondered. But my view was obscured.

"Lama, the box . . . It's empty," the groom whispered. He was confused.

Lama smiled. "Your marriage, like this box, is empty," he said.

The whole room stilled. I could feel the tenseness.

"If you put joy, openness, and kindness into your marriage, that's what you will get," Lama continued. "If you put anger, selfishness, and dishonesty into your marriage, that's also what you will get."

"Your life together starts now, so it's an empty box. You have the power to create any kind of marriage. Choose carefully what you put into it. May your life together be beautiful and beneficial!"

The tension lifted instantly as the room erupted in cheers.

The principles I've shared in this book are universal. If you apply them to other areas of your life, you'll see results in those areas too. By practicing these principles, you can change your destiny.

As you experience new dating adventures, drop me a line. Connect with me through Instagram (@patschang). Send me a message, or invite me to speak in your city.

I'd love to hear how you've uplifted your romantic life. Tell me about your adventures or how the lessons have transformed your life.

You can create a world that will amaze you in every way. Anything you can imagine, you can have. The principles are so powerful that I'm continually amazed.

As you practice what I've shared with you, you will begin to have your own adventures. Your dating doubts, disappointments, and bitterness will begin to fade, replaced by a sense of hope and possibility. Your dating life is unlimited and filled with possibilities.

You're a super quad dater. You get to rise in love, fulfill your dreams, and live head over wheels.

# ACKNOWLEDGMENTS

This book was created with love, support, encouragement, and gentle prodding from my wife, Antonia, and our son; my parents, Tony and Linda Chang; my siblings, Michelle Lin and Jeff Chang; my friends: Monte Lee, Steven Sim, Homan Igehy, Sepi Pashaie, Morris Twu, Gary Jackson, Elaine Wong, Sharon Lee-Thibault, Eric Wong, Master Lin, Joshua and Ivy Tan, Daniel Ku and Stella Hoh, Ein Li Chew, Ian Meredith, Chong Foo, Sinjin Lim, Nano Gazze, Rory Sutter, Ashley Johnson, Josephine Courant, James Thompson, Gavin Wright, Andrée Sursock, Mike Ivanitsky, Klaus Desmet, Sunit Mahajan, Klaus Daehne, Sara Lee Daehne, Michael Strass, Keith Bolshaw, Simone Milani, Tom Chun, Kevin V. Lowrey, Steve Dalton, Victor Su, and Evan Piper; and Helen Chang, Laurie Aranda, and the Author Bridge Media team.

# ABOUT THE AUTHOR

Pat Chang knows a lot about dating in a wheelchair—he's been in one since a diving accident when he was 13 left him paralyzed from the chest down, with limited use of his arms and hands. Before the accident, he was a competitive swimmer with washboard abs and straight-A grades. Popular and physically attractive, he knew that dating would be easy for him. But his accident not only took his athleticism—it took his confidence.

 @patschang

As much as Pat feared rejection and embarrassment, he dreaded being alone even more. So in his early twenties, he started to adapt classic dating rituals to work with his wheelchair. As he became less self-conscious and more self-assured, he discovered how to seduce women. But his relationships rarely lasted more than six months and inevitably left him feeling empty.

After yet another painful breakup, he asked himself, *Why don't my relationships work out? What's the common factor?*

Pat realized that he wasn't willing to show his true feelings because he was afraid to look weak. His problems stemmed not from his disability itself but from how he thought about his disability. He was always trying to hide or compensate for it. He let it dominate his dating life and determine his mindset.

This revelation prompted him to gradually, but painfully, let go of the bitter feelings about his disability. He realized that to have companionship, he needed to give companionship. As he adopted that lesson into his dating life, his relationships became more joyous and fulfilling. As he grew into a loving companion, he attracted a loving companion: Antonia, now his wife of many years.

Pat began to travel the world, sharing his story and inspiring millions of others to be head over wheels. Pat and his wife live in Singapore, where they continue to rise in love, and are currently planting seeds to double the size of their household.

 @patschang